20
MOST COMMON
TRADING
MISTAKES
AND HOW YOU CAN
AVOID THEM

KEL BUTCHER

Wrightbooks

First published 2009 by Wrightbooks
an imprint of John Wiley & Sons Australia, Ltd
42 McDougall Street, Milton Qld 4064
Office also in Melbourne

Typeset in Berkeley LT 11.3/14pt

National Library of Australia Cataloguing-in-Publication entry:

Author:	Butcher, Kel.
Title:	20 most common trading mistakes: and how you can avoid them/ Kel Butcher.
ISBN	9781742169293 (pbk.)
Notes:	Includes index.
Subjects:	Investments.
	Stock exchanges.
	Investment analysis.
Dewey Number:	332.02401

Cover image: © aispl, 2009. Used under license from Shutterstock.com.

Figures on pages 118–120: Microsoft Excel screen shot(s) reprinted with permission from Microsoft Corporation.

Printed in China by Printplus Limited
10 9 8 7 6 5 4 3 2 1

Disclaimer

Contents

There are no mistakes. The events we bring upon ourselves, no matter how unpleasant, are necessary in order to learn what we need to learn; whatever steps we take, they're necessary to reach the places we've chosen to go.

Richard Bach

Mistakes are the only universal form of originality.

Mason Cooley

It's not my fault — I didn't even know it was a mistake!

Mistake 1: defining a trading mistake

The greatest mistake you can make in life is to be continually fearing you will make one.

Elbert Hubbard, *The Note Book*, 1927

My guess is that most of you are probably inquisitive as to what constitutes a trading mistake. Given that this is a book about trading mistakes and how to avoid them, it seems only logical that the first chapter needs to define what mistakes are, and highlight some of the many mistakes that are discussed in the following pages.

Trading mistakes inevitably stem from two main sources: believing that trading is easy; and not having a well-defined plan for engaging the market. Invariably, all mistakes that traders make emanate from these two things. Much of this chapter is from an interview with leading market educator and world-renowned trading coach Dr Van Tharp, whose comments appear in bold throughout this chapter. He offers the following definition of a trading mistake:

A mistake can be defined in one of two ways:
1.   First, I consider it a mistake to make the assumption that trading or investing is easy and that you don't

need to do a lot of work to be successful. In fact, if people don't go through the five steps [outlined on page 3], then everything they do is probably a mistake. The second definition has to do with the results of the first step.

2.   It is a mistake to not follow a complete set of rules and guidelines as a trader; this should be written down in your working business plan. A mistake occurs when you break any of your rules.

A great pick-up line

The romantic notion and lure of trading attracts people to the promise of profit from buying and selling anything from shares in companies, through foreign exchange, to the global commodity markets. It is one of the last great free market activities available to anyone with a computer and a telephone. The entrepreneurial spirit in all of us is kindled by the thought of actively buying and selling gold futures, currencies and a wide range of other markets. It also makes great cocktail party conversation when people enquire as to what you do: 'Oh, not much', you reply casually, 'I'm a trader'. Instantly a world of fast cars, glamorous people and sailing in Monaco flashes before their eyes. Little do they realise that the reality of trading is brutally different from this glossy, shallow image portrayed in the marketing hype of many of the lesser respected promoters in this industry. It takes persistent hard work to become a consistently successful trader.

Trading is a profession like any other. Most people go through many years of schooling and training to learn their profession, but not for trading. Entry is easy—just open up a brokerage account. It is comparable to the average person walking into a hospital and telling the staff, 'I'd like to practise brain surgery today'. If they'd allow it (as they do trading), then the results probably would be fatal to the patient just as the results in trading are usually fatal to your account if you are one of the typically ill-prepared traders. *The first major mistake people make is not having the appropriate training.*

There are five steps people should go through to get the training they need before engaging the market:

1. Extensive self-examination and working through psychological issues. This is an ongoing process that never truly ends, but I'm willing to say that most people have completed this step when they have solved five major psychological issues. For example, someone might say, 'My self-esteem is low and I have a lot of anger because my father always used to criticise me and put me down. However, I've worked on my anger through various feeling-release techniques and now it seldom comes up'. When people have solved five issues, I think that they can handle most other things that come up and are ready to move on to step two. *Not knowing your common patterns and how you might self-sabotage is a major mistake.*

2. Develop a working business plan to guide you through the trading process. This should include a statement of who you are (resulting from step one); objectives; an assessment of the big picture; at least three trading systems that fit the big picture; a complete set of business systems (like how to do research, how to manage data, and so on); a worst-case contingency plan; position sizing strategies to meet objectives (these would be a subset of the systems); and a psychological management plan. *Being ill-prepared for the unexpected is also a major mistake.*

3. You need several non-correlated systems that fit the big picture. One of the biggest mistakes that people make is to develop one trading system and then try to fit it to all market types. You cannot do it. But you can design a really good system, perhaps even a Holy Grail–type system to fit any particular market. For example, there is a huge difference between a quiet bull market and a hugely volatile bear market, or even a hugely volatile sideways market. And all three markets probably need different systems. You need to understand how to look at market type (in a way that

fits how you trade) and only trade markets in which your system works well. *Trading without a system (defined below) is a mistake. Not knowing how your system will perform in each market type is a major mistake.*

4. You need a great set of objectives that fit who you are and then you need a position sizing™ strategy that fits your objectives. Position sizing is that part of your strategy that tells you how much to risk throughout the course of the trade. Most people don't realise (again a mistake) that it is through position sizing that you meet your objectives. A great system just makes it easier to meet your objectives through position sizing. Not having objectives is a mistake. *Not having a position sizing algorithm designed to meet your objectives is also a mistake.*

5. You need to monitor your trading to minimise the impact of mistakes. This shows that, if you've completed all five steps, a mistake only results from not following your rules. *Not having a plan in place to monitor and correct your mistakes also is a mistake.*

How much did that cost?

When all is said and done, mistakes cost us money—either through not exiting a losing trade at a predefined stop-loss point, not taking trades according to the rules of our trading system due to some arbitrary or emotional influence on our thinking, or just doing things that should never be considered as viable or sensible trading decisions in the first place. All traders need to identify the point at which they accept defeat and cut losing trades as well as a way to monitor their overall performance based on the extent of these losses.

One of the cardinal rules of good trading is to always have an exit point before you enter into a trade. *Not having an exit point is another mistake.* This is your worst-case risk for the trade. It's the point at which you would say, 'Something's wrong with this trade and I need to get out to preserve my capital'. Your initial stop defines your initial risk, which I call 1R (where R stands for risk). If you know your initial risk, then you can express all of your results in terms of your initial risk.

Say that your initial risk is $10 per share on a $40 stock. If you make a profit of $50 per share, then you have a gain of 5R. If you have a loss of $15 per share, then you have a 1.5R loss. Losses bigger than 1R will occur when you have a sudden big move against you.

Let's look at a few more. If the stock goes up to $140, what's your profit in terms of R? Your profit is $100 and your initial risk is $10, so you've made a 10R profit. It's quite interesting because portfolio managers like to talk about 10-baggers. A 10-bagger means a stock bought at $10 per share that goes up to $100 — in other words, a stock that goes up in value 10 times. However, I think a 10R gain is much more useful to think about and much easier to attain. When our 1R was $10 per share, then the stock had to go up by $100 to get a 10R gain. But to fit the portfolio manager's definition of a 10-bagger, it would have had to go up 10 times the price you bought it for, going from $40 per share to $400. But the $360 gain in terms of R-multiples when your initial risk was $10 would be a 36R gain!

Thus, another cardinal rule is to have profits that are many times your initial risk. *When you take a trade, if you don't think you can make at least 2R (3R is better), then you are probably making another mistake.* Your profits and losses should always be stated as some multiple of your initial risk, which I call an R-multiple.

In my opinion a trading system is defined by the distribution of the R-multiples that it generates. From that distribution, you can get a mean (average) value which is the expectancy of the system. If a system has an expectancy of 0.8R, on average over many trades, you'll make 80 per cent of your initial risk in your trading system. *Having a system that doesn't generate a positive expectancy is also another major mistake — so is not knowing the expectancy of your system.*

Now that you know about R and R-multiples, you can also start thinking about mistakes in terms of R-values and that's where we've been doing some research.

Analyse to understand

I've been asking the traders that I coach to keep track of their mistakes in terms of R. For example, if you enter the market on emotion and you make 2R, then that counts as +2R towards that mistake. If you do it again and you lose 4R, you now have -2R towards that mistake. If you do that for about a year, you'll have a good idea about how efficient you are as a trader and what your efficiency costs you.

One of my clients was a futures trader, running a $200 million account. We estimated that over nine months he made 11 mistakes, costing him 46.5R. Thus, he made 1.2 mistakes per month, costing him 4.23R per mistake. Overall, his profit was probably 50 per cent less than it could have been because of mistakes. If he made 20 per cent profit, he probably could have made 70 per cent profit. Now can you begin to see the impact of such mistakes?

Another client was a long-term position trader, primarily trading exchange traded funds (ETFs) with wide stops. In a year of trading, he made 27 mistakes costing him 8.2R. Thus, over a year he made 2.25 mistakes per month. However, because he was trading long term with large stops and no leverage, his mistakes were not as costly. Each mistake was costing him 0.3R. During the year of trading he was up 31R (and about 30 per cent). Had he not made any mistakes, he would have been up 39.2R. His mistakes cost him 20 per cent of his profits.

What are your mistakes costing you?

Oops, sorry, my mistake

Mistakes generally fit into two main categories: one broadly relating to overall market interaction; the other relating to everyday operational mistakes. A third category, execution errors, is also discussed in chapter 19.

The first main mistake category are 'global' mistakes — such as not having a trading system and not having a working business plan. Most of the types of errors I've mentioned so far are global mistakes.

The second category includes the types of mistakes where people break specific rules. Here are some of the most common that I've documented:

- Entering on a tip, an emotion or something that doesn't correspond to one of your well-considered systems.
- Not exiting when you should be stopped out.
- Risking too much money on any given trade.
- Doing anything because of an emotional reaction, including exiting too soon.
- Not following your daily routine.
- Blaming someone or something for what happens to you rather than accepting personal responsibility.
- Trading multiple systems in the same account.
- Trading so many trades in the same account that you cannot keep track of them.
- Trading a system when the market type has changed and you know the system will now perform poorly.
- Concentrating on the entry for a system and not the potential reward-to-risk ratio in the trade.
- Taking a profit too quickly or not taking a loss just to be 'right' or prove a point.
- Not having a predetermined exit when you enter the trade.
- Not keeping track of the R-multiples and the general performance of your trading system.

Of course, there are many more mistakes. The more common ones are detailed in this book.

Prevention is better than cure

The good news is that mistakes can be avoided. Through appropriate training and education, including reading this book, you can learn how to avoid the mistakes that the vast majority of people make. If you take the time to learn from the experiences of the contributors to this book, you will be a long way down the road of avoiding many of these mistakes. You can also practise not making mistakes through daily positive reinforcement of a non-mistake making belief system.

I recommend that at the beginning of each day you go through a process called mental rehearsal. Ask yourself, 'What could go wrong today that might cause me to make a mistake?' Suppose you have nothing to do because you'll either be in your positions or get stopped out. Thus, you might decide that the only thing you might do that would be a mistake is to override your stops. For example, you might hear some guru on the television making comments on some stock you own and decide to sell and not keep your stop.

So when you come up with that particular idea, you rehearse how to avoid it. You could turn the television off. You could watch the television without any sound if you must look at charts and prices. Or you could go through some procedure where you neutralise any comments that are said about stocks you currently own.

The market always presents us with events that one would probably never imagine. We've recently had market volatility that is 10 standard deviations bigger than the norm. That has almost a zero probability of occurring if market volatility were normally distributed, but it is occurring. If you are not prepared to trade in this sort of climate, it could be a disaster.

Similarly, who could have imagined that the US stock market would actually close for a while because the World Trade Center was destroyed? Did you predict that one?

I recommend that everyone do a daily mental rehearsal by asking, 'What could go wrong today to cause me to make a mistake?' Become creative and think of everything. For everything you come up with, rehearse how you'll perform to make sure that it doesn't have a significant impact upon your trading.

One day you might meet that big losing trade in the markets that has your number on it. Wouldn't it be a good idea to be prepared for it ahead of time? If you make one mistake in every 10 trades, then you are 90 per cent efficient as a trader. Increasing your efficiency from 90 per cent (that is, one mistake every 10 trades) to 98 per cent (that is, one mistake every 50 trades) could actually double your return rate or more.

First time it's a mistake, second time it's my fault, third time I'm an idiot

As well as being financially costly and emotionally devastating, repeating any mistake more than once is just plain stupid. But it need not be a part of your psyche if you choose to not make the mistake again, and if you choose to work through a process to review mistakes to ensure they do not recur.

Repeating the same mistake over and over again is a form of self-sabotage. And it's one that anyone should be able to understand. At the end of each trading day, I recommend that you take a minute to review your trading and ask yourself, 'Did I make any mistakes?' If you didn't, even if you lost money, then pat yourself on the back. You actually did well.

If you made a mistake, then look at the situation that led to the mistake. What happened that you need to look out for in the future? This is probably a mistake that you did not deal with in your mental rehearsal. You need to mentally rehearse the situation to make sure that you don't repeat the mistake. Rehearsing your solution in your conscious mind several times puts it into your unconscious mind and helps you make an automatic response in the heat of the moment during the trade.

By the way, the daily debriefing and the initial mental rehearsal are two of my top tasks of trading that people should do each day. And you can probably see how valuable they are. Not doing them every trading day is another mistake—of the global variety.

Avoiding the blame game

Just like in life, trading is all about taking responsibility for every single decision and action you make. In the words of renowned trader and respected market educator Larry Williams, 'trading is life personified'. You can get on with it, take responsibility for all your actions, and enjoy what you do, knowing that every decision you make along the way is yours to keep, and that you accept the responsibility for everything you do and everything that happens. You are 100 per cent accountable to yourself and others for all your actions. Or you can blame anyone else that happens to be even slightly associated with any of the negative outcomes that occur throughout life.

> The most important trait that any trader needs is personal responsibility. It means that somehow you caused your results. For example, in our marble game, which teaches people the importance of position sizing, I use a bag of marbles to simulate a trading system. I typically use a system that is wrong about 80 per cent of the time so that we have big losing streaks but big R-multiple winners. The marbles are replaced after each trade so that the odds are always the same. My game typically has an expectancy of 0.8R and easily could have 10 consecutive losers in a game of 40 trades. Typically, you need to survive the 10 losses in a row to get the long-term expectancy, which is usually around 32R by the end of the game.
>
> However, I usually have the same person pull out a marble (and then replace it) until that person pulls out a winning marble. Thus, any long losing streak in the game will be associated with one person. At the end of the game, I can ask of the people who

went bankrupt, 'How many of you think you went bankrupt or lost money because of this person?' as I point to the person who was associated with the long losing streak. Many hands will go up; that's what I call blame.

People go bankrupt when they practise poor position sizing. That's the mistake. If you recognise this, then you are taking personal responsibility and you can fix the mistake. However, if you blame the person who pulled out the marbles, or the trading system itself, then you are not taking responsibility and you'll probably repeat the mistake over and over again.

So people need the personal responsibility to recognise how they created their results, because it's the only way they can be improved.

If you blame someone or something, it doesn't fix anything: 'It's his fault'; 'It's a terrible trading system'. If you justify, it doesn't fix anything: 'It's a stupid game'; 'It doesn't count'; 'It doesn't resemble real trading at all'; 'It's just luck and I was unlucky'. And even if you blame yourself, it doesn't fix anything: 'I'm a stupid idiot who keeps getting bad breaks'.

You must have the trait of always looking for how you produced your results. And when you do, then you can fix mistakes.

As a trader, you must take responsibility and accept that every action — win, lose or draw — is a result of your actions and decisions. If you can't or won't accept this, close this book now and go back to your day job — it's that important.

Remember that average doesn't cut it. It takes a lot of work to be good. You put a lot of work into learning your profession. Why do people think trading or investing should take anything less? Instead, follow the five steps that I recommended earlier.

Trading coach and author **Dr Van K Tharp** is widely recognised for his best-selling books, *Trade Your Way to Financial Freedom* and *The Definitive Guide to Position Sizing*, plus his outstanding Peak

Performance Home Study Program—a highly regarded classic that is suitable for all levels of traders and investors. You can learn more about Van Tharp, sign up for his free e-newsletter and download his trading simulation game at <www.vantharp.com>.

The horse goes in front of the cart

Mistake 2: jumping into the market before having learned the required skills

Human beings, who are almost unique in having the ability to learn from the experience of others, are also remarkable for their apparent disinclination to do so.

Douglas Adams

'How much money will I make?', 'Will I be a successful and profitable trader by next week?', 'How long does all this take?' As a trader, coach and mentor I have lost count of the amount of times I have been asked these and similar questions. All revolve around the central theme of being able to trade profitably with a minimum level of learning and preparation and the ill-conceived notion that success and profit will flow effortlessly. The questions come from a broad range of intending traders, from successful self-employed business owners, engineers and doctors, to those who have held a government job for 40 years and now somehow believe that they are going to become successful traders overnight.

The industry itself has much to do with creating the illusion that success as a trader is our democratic right, living as we do in a capitalist world. Many trading educators, commentators and supposed 'gurus' build their business around encouraging all and sundry to participate in the wonderful world of trading where profits are generated while you sleep or go fishing with your mates. They also paint a picture of trading as an occupation that requires little work or effort, merely a computer and 10 minutes a day to generate wealth beyond the realms of imagination. It's a hoax! As you will read throughout this book, success in any trading endeavour requires dedication, commitment and lots of hard work. It is not an easy business, but one that requires discipline and a consistent application of a well-researched trading plan, coupled with a complete understanding and acceptance of the range of probabilities associated with any strategy.

The role of reputable market educators is important to the successful development of a profitable trading business. The trick is to seek out the 'real' ones. Find the traders with years of experience, not those with the latest whiz-bang indicator with promises of easy returns and early retirement for little or no work. Experienced traders have a realistic rate of profitable return over an extended period of time.

Market educator and seminar organiser David Hunt has been involved with a wide range of reputable market educators for many years. He has been responsible for arranging some of the world's high-profile traders and educators to teach and train people in Australia. David offers his views on the role of these professionals in educating those who want to become successful traders.

> Most traders start out not knowing anything at all. They have no experience in trading. The only thing they have is capital and a dream of making money (easy or otherwise) that has been fuelled by an ad they have read promising them quick money and an easy way to enter the trading world. They may have been good business people or successful professionals but the skills required for successful trading are way different. Good trading requires not adding money to a losing position whereas sometimes in business recapitalisation is needed to ensure survival and success.
>
> The role of market educators is to give traders a look at what is possible in trading for them to see what strategies, methods and rules there are for trading markets. It's a lower risk

opportunity to try before they risk their real money. A trainee pilot is given procedures to follow. A trainee surgeon is given the knowledge and support of previous doctors. Yet trainee traders think they will jump into the market after having read one book or attending one dodgy seminar and make a squillion dollars in about five days.

Good market educators share their knowledge and experience and their rules that they have proven over time that work. In other words, market educators give a structured way of dealing with the great unknown of where the market is going and how to make money from it.

Beginner traders can luck into a 2003 to 2007 bull market with no knowledge and clean up through good luck rather than any particular level of skill. But when the bear market hits they lose all they made and then some. They have to pay the piper sometime. These people will often seek education and help after they have lost large sums of money. More often than not, they have made huge profits during a bull market and then given it all back, plus a chunk of their original capital, when the market conditions change, because they do not know how to limit risk. They have profited off the back of a rising market, but have never bothered to develop the skills necessary to trade through a variety of market conditions.

Good market educators teach you how to limit risk and take positive expectation trades. They give traders a structured way and a realistic process for trading that could take many years and hundreds of thousands of dollars in time, money and trading losses to develop. They are happy to share their methods and processes with others because they know they work and they have nothing to hide.

Building from the ground up

It is important to learn and understand all aspects of the markets before you start trading. It's common knowledge that any enterprise is only as good as the foundations on which it is built, and trading is no different. If you take the time to learn and understand the workings of the markets, market conditions, interactions, trading styles and techniques, and market and personal psychology before engaging the markets you will have built a very solid foundation upon which to build your trading business. Too often potential traders jump into the market before they are properly prepared and the results are disastrous.

> The market is a magical thing, really. The markets give us the opportunity to make or lose a lot of money and play out all of our psychological issues and games in the blink of an eye or click of a mouse button.
>
> If you have deep-seated personal issues they will come out in trading. Markets are all mass psychology: fear, hope and greed. One minute you can feel like a hero, the next minute a complete loser.
>
> In simple terms, the market transfers money from the hands of the weak to the hands of the strong. If you do not understand the market, you put yourself in a position of weakness. You do not want to be weak in the markets. What you need to learn is a process of analysis and rules to follow that work in the long run across differing market conditions. But not all market conditions — no trading strategy will work in all market conditions. Traders need to learn what market conditions work for their strategies. They need to learn *one does not have to be right all the time to be a profitable trader*. For example, I was a director of a Turtle Trading Fund by original Turtle Trader, Russell Sands (see chapter 6). The Turtle method is very profitable in the long run. In 2008 the Turtle program made a profit of just under 200 per cent for the full year. Yet it lost about 53 per cent of the time on its trades. This method has only had one losing year out of 25 years.

Teaching the old dogs new tricks

Training and education is a vital part of initially learning about the markets and the actual activity of trading. Ongoing training and skill development is also important. The markets are always changing and new markets and products are continually being added to the range of options open to traders. The rapid expansion of both the contract for difference (CFD) market and the foreign exchange (Forex) market are testimony to this. It is estimated that in excess of $3 trillion is traded daily on the Forex markets, up from under $2 trillion in 2004. This is a 71 per cent surge in daily volume in three years. To participate in these markets and to take advantage of the opportunities they present, education and training is required, even by those who may have been trading other instruments for years.

Each market has it nuances and idiosyncrasies that need to be learned and understood if one is to trade them successfully, so ongoing education is an essential requirement for those who wish to successfully participate in these markets. The temptation to jump into trading before being adequately prepared exists just as much for some experienced traders as it does for those starting out on their trading career. The age-old issues of greed, fear and hope strangle our logical thought processes and convince us that we had better 'get in quick' before we miss the next great opportunity that will be a massive winning trade. This thinking usually results in jumping into the markets when ill-prepared and unready for the range of outcomes that the markets can and will throw up. The next emotion is panic as we realise that we have no idea what to do next, and then emotional turmoil and financial loss as the whole thing goes drastically wrong. If we had taken the time to be fully prepared and not risked jumping in too early for fear of missing out, then no doubt the experience would be dramatically different.

Patience is a virtue

The old saying that 'there will be another bus leaving the station in a few minutes' can be applied time and again for those wishing to jump into trading before they are adequately prepared. All too often, particularly in a rampaging bull market, underprepared traders are busting to jump into the market to grab a slice of the pie they think they are missing out on. Fuelled by stories in the press—from their mates, work colleagues, or anyone else with an opinion—of the huge profits people are making 'trading', they become fearful of missing out or of being left behind in the rush. These people grab onto the latest fad or trading seminar that promises them a slice of the action and away they go.

Fired up on adrenalin and just enough information to be dangerous, they launch headfirst into their trading career. Swept along by the wave of euphoria, they usually experience some success and become complacent at the 'ease' of trading. With little (if any) awareness of risk and money management, underprepared traders are struck by the greed mistress and their position sizes and risk profile become misaligned with their abilities. Suddenly, and without warning, the market changes and they are blown out of the water by the speed and severity of this attack on their abilities. Under siege, they panic. With no notes in their instruction manual, they self-destruct and suffer a devastating psychological and financial blow.

In stark contrast with this are those who have learned their skills from an educator who has not only shown them a few entry and exit techniques, but has also stressed money management, position sizing and risk management skill development, and has encouraged them to develop their own individual trading style. These guys are armed with the tools necessary to not only survive, but to perhaps prosper when markets turn. They have learned the importance of stop losses, manageable position sizes and managing the emotions of fear and greed. They understand the concepts of developing a trader's mindset and thinking in terms of probabilities. They are educated, prepared and know what they will do and how they will do it under a variety of market conditions.

Choosing the shoe that fits

Not all market educators are the same. The industry ranges from the slick salesman with the well-oiled marketing plan of a seminar or system with little substance and a high price tag, to the low-key professional trader who may not have the slickest presentation skills but whose methods and techniques have a solid track record and are well proven in a real-time trading environment.

From my experience, there are four main types of market educators, as described below.

The McDonald's corporate style school

The *McDonald's corporate style* trading education is formulaic education at high prices, usually taught by junior staff who never seem to have the same trades on as their students. Most students start here and have no money left over after paying tuition.

When you talk with their brokers you discover that these students are net losers with the exception of some spectacular, well-publicised winners who are invariably overtrading. You will see lots of flashy ads in papers and on TV for these 'educators'.

The basic trading methodology will slowly lose money. When the crowd all trades one way then the crowd will be wrong. In fact, professional traders often buy these systems just to do the opposite of the recommended trades. Most of the educators are teaching the same stuff—it's the market where no-one makes money.

The space cadet secret knowledge school

The *space cadet secret knowledge school* relies on mystery, secret formulas and magical indicators. In the end, some do not teach you how to trade at all. They just show you how to apply these apparent secrets and charge you an exorbitant fee for the privilege. They are very good marketers and have loud voices.

The 'I'm rich; you can be too' school

The *'I'm rich; you can be too! Just do my course'* school is run by guys giving long and repetitive presentations. They teach you zip about trading but tell you how they are an astronaut or deep-sea diver adventurer. They usually promote options trading because it is leveraged and the returns look more spectacular when compared with margin and outlay. When you talk with the brokers, these students are break-even traders on the whole. They are wonderful at showing you all their past successes and historical trades on hand-picked charts. They show you lots of winning trades and hardly ever display a losing trade.

The individual real trader school

The *individual real trader school* does not have glossy advertising or a series of promotional media ads. Their stands at trading expos tend to be low-key and lack the glitz and glamour of the types mentioned above. They are traders and authors who actually trade their methods as well as teach. They are prepared to disclose and teach you their methods and also how to think and research the markets and come up with trading ideas for yourself (that is, to become independent). These real traders will openly and honestly discuss winning trades, losing trades, drawdowns, and every other aspect of their trading style and the markets. Their goal is to help you learn and understand the markets and then to apply your own skills to become an independent and successful trader.

Reality check required

The promises of miraculous returns for little or no work are the dreams of the ill-informed and uneducated trader. If a market educator is promising some amazing return from a secret 'system' that is only available to a select few at a greatly inflated price, then run for the hills. It will simply not work over the long term. Look for educators who not only teach you their trading style, but from whom you can learn the necessary skills and mindset to develop your own unique trading style that suits you!

Too much pressing the greed button through marketing and overselling the dream is a red flag and should immediately raise your suspicions as to the real beneficiary of you attending the advertised training. Will you benefit from the learning and knowledge gained, or will the 'guru' who has never taken a real trade benefit more by taking your cash?

The real guys will often teach and trade at the same time. Actually, trading in front of people is much harder than trading in your own office. This is a sign they believe in what they do—you can also see if they follow their own rules.

In this chapter, David Hunt, founding member and president of the Australian Technical Analysts Association (ATAA), gave his take on getting properly prepared to start trading any market.

David freely admits he had to forget his education as an economist in order to make money trading the markets. His trading career began in foreign exchange in 1986 working for a large Australian listed company. He then worked as a proprietary trader for a large bank before managing a large Australian bond fund. During this time David began teaching other traders both trading skills and money management. He is a founding member and the current president of the Australian Technical Analysts Association. In 1996 David founded the boutique market education firm ADEST (<www.adest.com.au>), bringing many high-profile traders to Australia.

He is a consultant to advanced financial planning firms in asset allocation, market timing and share selection.

Failing to plan is planning to fail

Mistake 3: not having a clearly defined and documented trading plan

Without goals and plans to achieve them, you are like
a ship that has set sail without a destination.

Anon.

As a trader or investor, the need to have a well-researched and documented plan, or set of rules, for engaging any market is paramount to success. This applies regardless of your chosen time frame or chosen market. The necessity of a trading plan applies to day traders just as much as it applies to longer term share investors. It is a common theme that is stressed by all of the interviewees in this book. Each and every one of them has a plan for engaging the market and has a written set of rules that specify the plan regardless of their trading time frame or chosen market.

From Davin Clarke (see chapter 7) trading extremely short-term moves on Australian shares and derivatives, to Russell Sands (see chapter 6) trading long-term trend moves in the commodity markets — all of these professional traders have a written trading plan that specifies in detail every aspect of their trading strategy. Those trading multiple strategies across multiple markets, such as

Jake Bernstein (see chapter 12), will have a plan for each of these, plus an overall set of rules which includes details of their maximum risk exposure and other money management and risk management parameters.

Write it down

Australian trader Justine Pollard, author of the book *Smart Trading Plans*, offers these words of advice to those setting out to document their trading plan:

> Every trading plan is personal and individual and you need to document your own rules for all aspects of your trading business—what may suit one trader will not necessarily suit another. As a trader, you are totally responsible for your own decisions and actions in the market, so your plan needs to be unique. It needs to reflect your personal motivations for trading and be based on a method that suits your personality and lifestyle. This will be influenced by how much time you have to devote to trading, the amount of available capital you have to trade, and your personal risk profile.
>
> You need to include everything about your trading business in your plan, from your goals, to your trading system right up to all worst-case scenarios. Following is a quick summary of the main areas that need to be covered in any trading plan for someone serious about their trading business.
>
> ⤷ *Goals and objectives*—consider why you want to be a trader and what you want to achieve. Create a vision around trading.
>
> ⤷ *Trading structure*—decide if you will trade under your own personal name (which you might start with) or a business structure, such as a company, trust, partnership or even self-manage your super fund and take control of your investments.
>
> ⤷ *Trading tools*—what are all the tools that you will use to trade the market: website, newspapers, magazines,

brokers, newsletters, software programs and data sources?

⇨ *Trading style*—do you want to be a day trader, short-term trader of a few days or a week, medium-term trader of a week to a few months, or long-term trader of months to years?

⇨ *Trading indicators*—what indicators will you use to help your trading decisions? Will it be technical indicators, such as moving averages, RSI, MACD, ATR, stochastic, and so on, or fundamental indicators such as P/E ratios and dividend yields?

⇨ *Order execution*—will you use a full-service broker to place your buy and sell orders, or will you trade from an online platform and execute all the orders yourself?

⇨ *Trade exit rules*—this will include: initial stop-loss criteria; rules for trailing stops; profit targets or trend-following rules; if and when you will pyramid into positions; and if you will use a time-based rule to exit trades that are just drifting.

⇨ *Risk and money management*—this is the most important part of your trading plan and is the only control you have over the market. It determines how you open the trade with a position sizing methodology and how you will manage the trade once it is open through a stop-loss strategy. It also guides how you will track and set a heat level to manage your maximum drawdown at any point in the market. It will also include details of when you will increase position size as your account value increases and when you will reduce position sizes if your account suffers a string of losses.

⇨ *Market exposure guidelines*—how you plan to expose yourself to the market after a cluster of losses or when the market trend changes.

⇨ *Trading systems*—this is your set-up and trigger criteria for selecting trades and your specific exit strategy and management plan for each trade. Will these systems be ones you design and build yourself, learn from someone else and adapt for your own use, or a commercially available system that you buy or lease from a system vendor?

⇨ *Trading routine*—what do you plan to do on a daily, weekly and quarterly basis to analyse the market, select shares and manage your trades?

⇨ *Trading performance and analysis*—you need to regularly evaluate your performance as a trader and understand how your trading business is performing and if you need to take any specific action if things are not going well. This will include performance parameters for your trading systems based on all the relevant numbers, and perhaps for yourself based on personal parameters such as stress levels, time to take a holiday, and so on.

⇨ *Contingency plan for all worst-case scenarios*—consider all things that could go wrong with your trading business and have a plan for how to handle these if they were to occur.

The need to have rules for trading becomes even more important during 'tough' times and periods of uncertainty. During buoyant times when markets are trending up and trading appears an easy way to make money, rules are forgotten and traders become slack in applying their rules, if they have even bothered to create a structured set of rules or approach. During such market phases, with steadily rising prices and continued good news forever emanating from all sources, mistakes are often covered by the constant upward push of prices. Stops are forgotten about, position sizing models go out the window, and entry and exit rules become haphazard and slack. Talk to the average punter during these times and the majority will have never considered a plan for trading, let alone documented rules. Easy money is made listening to tips from various sources, trading by 'gut' feel, and even just haphazardly buying and selling based on news snippets and rumours.

Only fools have no rules

It all ends in tears when the tide turns and prices crash, a down-trending bear market begins, or the market goes into a long period of sideways consolidation where prices chop around within a range. The reckless punters are left battered and bruised and wondering where the train came from that just slammed into them at 100 kilometres an hour, knocking them and their bank accounts backwards. However, the professional traders and investors have exited their long positions and are now profiting from the move occurring in the opposite direction. They have been able to do this through being educated and running their trading enterprise as a professional business, and predominantly through the use of a written set of rules for all aspects of their market activities. Their trading plans have allowed them to exit trades cleanly and decisively without any conjecture or agonising over what to do. The decisions are made almost clinically as they are taken out of trades on profit targets or stops, and they exit these trades without fear or any emotional attachment. Meanwhile, the punters are agonising over their decisions and watching portfolios get decimated by a relentless downtrend. They continue to look for any reasons to justify why they are still in a losing trade. They will cling to any useless piece of information that appears to justify this lack of activity and inability to get out of these losing trades.

Transfer the funds to my account, please

Markets will always separate the professional or prepared trader from the unprepared. They will also continue to transfer money and wealth from the unprepared to the prepared. Sometimes it takes a while, sometimes not so long. The huge worldwide surge in equity prices in the four years up to late 2007, followed by the huge and continuing downtrend in 2008, is such an example. The years of extended upward moving equity prices led to complacency and neglect of the usual discipline for many traders. Prices seemed to be in a never-ending upward movement. The eagerness to participate in this move and not get left behind was further precipitated by relentless news stories (see chapter 14). This continually talked prices up and encouraged people to buy, buy, buy as the mega-cycle of rising prices was 'set to continue for years' and we would all be multimillionaires by buying shares, particularly in mining and resource stocks supposedly fuelled by China's insatiable demand for these resources. On the back of this, all sorts of people were drawn to the share market. Their buying decisions were based on almost everything but a well-researched plan. Broker advice, newspaper stories, hot tips from mates, lunar cycles, dreams, anything and everything became fair game for buying shares. The majority of these people had little or any idea of what they were really doing, and what was really happening. And then it all went sour, as shown in figure 3.1.

Figure 3.1: chart of the 2003–2007 bull market and the 2008 crash

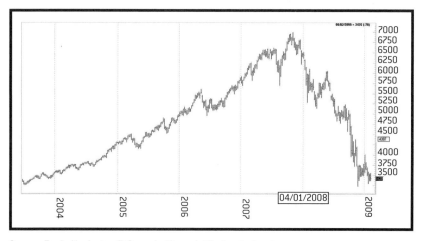

Source: Trade Navigator © Genesis Financial Technologies, Inc

The prepared and disciplined traders and investors knew what to do. They had a predefined set of rules that had been documented well in advance of the events that unfolded. They knew at what point they were to exit any long trades and open positions, and they did so swiftly and decisively. They were prepared. Then there were the unprepared—those who had no idea what had happened or what they now needed to do. They simply sat stunned and inert as prices crashed and their beloved shares were decimated at the hands of the bear market. They watched as portfolios halved in value and some companies that were once the darlings of the market were wiped out, taking them down with them. An example is shown in figure 3.2.

Figure 3.2: ABC Learning share price, 2002–2008

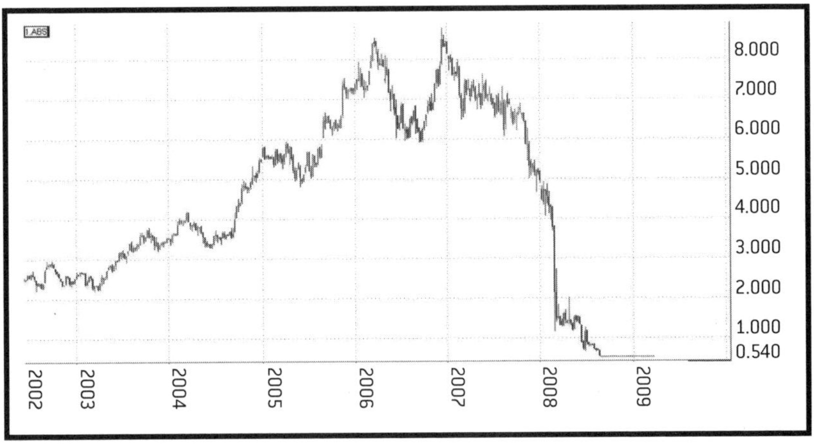

Source: Market Master

The prepared traders were now also short selling and profiting from the downtrend. Their trading plans contained rules for now trading in the opposite direction to the one they had been trading in for the past several years. To these traders, there was no difference. They simply took the short sell signals, again without emotional attachment or subjective reasoning, and got on with the business of trading. They made no judgement call on the rationale behind this sudden change in sentiment or direction, and had no reason to do so. They simply executed the trades according to the rules of their system or trading plan and continued playing by their rules to successfully and profitably engage the equity markets.

It took a while, but the wealth created by the unprepared was eventually transferred to the prepared. Those who had been complacent during the supposedly never-ending bull market for equities and super-cycle of commodity prices were smashed up on the rocks. Their lack of a professional approach to trading had cost them dearly. Those who had scoffed at the need for a trading plan and had blindly entered the markets on a whim were now lamenting this decision, searching for someone else to blame and crying into their beers to anyone who would listen to their stories of self-pity and grief. They had broken the number one rule of successfully running any business: have a plan. Without a plan they had no idea what to do when things went bad. During the good times they had simply ridden the coat-tails of the market in general and had been able to profit by doing this. As the saying goes, 'a rising tide lifts all boats'. When the market turned against them, they had no idea of what to do, and many of their sources for hot tips and advice had now either disappeared or changed their tune.

This prolonged fall in equity markets, brought about by what is being termed the 'global financial crisis', is an extreme example of what can happen when markets turn. But it is not an isolated incident. Corrections, price changes, outside influences and a huge array of factors are constantly bombarding markets. Figure 3.3 shows the huge upward move in oil prices during 2007 as speculation became rife that the world was running out of crude oil and prices would reach well above $200 per barrel, with some so-called experts even predicting it would reach $400 per barrel. It seems somehow that they were wrong!

Figure 3.3: crude oil price chart

Source: Trade Navigator © Genesis Financial Technologies, Inc.

Trades are constantly being entered and exited on a huge variety of markets all around the globe, 24 hours per day via electronic markets and trading platforms. Everywhere are woeful tales of someone being affected by this, that or the other reason in one or more of their trades, and how such-and-such announcement or event somehow had a catastrophic impact on their position. The vast majority of these stories emanate from those with no written trading plan or set of structured rules for engaging the markets they are trading.

Do it now

The best time to document your trading plan is *before* you begin trading. It is a task that requires discipline and commitment to complete it—not unlike trading itself. If you have the discipline to take the time to commit your trading plan to paper, the chances are much higher that you will succeed as a trader because you will be creating a disciplined and structured approach to all your trading activities.

Because it is a big task to complete a trading plan, it's easy to put it off and say 'I'll do it later', but it is a lot of information to carry around in your head. By taking this information out of your head and writing it down, you are giving your trading perspective, focus and clear guidelines. Plus, you are relieving your mind of the stress of trying to retain all that information and allowing more knowledge to come in. It is well worth the effort and you will feel much more at ease as you move forward with your trading.

It should be written before you even start trading. But most people have already traded in some way before even contemplating writing a trading plan. It is like a journey you go through. You start out just wanting to trade and wanting to get your money in the market and seeing dollar signs flashing in front of your eyes (I know I did). Then you take losses and your ego takes a beating and you either stop trading altogether or you get it together and realise you need to learn, educate yourself and write a trading plan—which I think is what happens to most people.

If you are trading and haven't committed a plan to paper then do it now! It will unburden your mind and provide you with a degree of clarity for your trading that you may not currently have.

> It is a huge feeling of relief, like a weight lifted off your shoulders, when you complete your trading plan. It is hard work and takes time to do, but it feels so good when it is complete and the benefits are endless. You will now have clear rules and guidelines to follow and have answered all the 'what if?'s.
>
> It also gives your trading clarity and control. You can't control the market, it does not know you exist, but you can control how you manage your risk in the market and that is so important. Your plan should include clear risk and money management strategies and this is what will give you control over your trading.

It's evolutionary, baby

Your trading plan will be a constantly evolving document. Like a living organism, it will grow, expand and change with you as you develop as a trader. While it is important to know exactly what your rules of engagement are, it is also important to realise that these will change over time. For example, you may move from trading shares to trading futures. Changes to some markets or regulatory controls imposed by ill-informed rule makers may force you to adjust the markets you trade or the instruments you use to trade these markets. Your lifestyle may change as a result of shifting family circumstances, such as children entering your life. Life is a constant state of ebb and flow as a huge variety of external forces effect the way we trade, the time and capital we have available, and the markets we can or want to trade. This flexibility is just as important as the discipline of writing down your trading plan. The most important thing to do is recognise and document these changes in your trading plan so you know exactly what it is you are doing all of the time.

> Anybody who plans to invest money in the market needs a trading plan. Think about it, if you were to buy a business, would you buy it without analysing it and understanding its costs, profit

potential, drawdowns, worst-case scenarios and working out a plan to market it? Trading is no different and should be treated the same way.

When you trade the markets, you are putting money at risk with the goal of achieving a profit, just like any small business. So you need to treat it like a business and have a plan that sets out how you are going to manage it.

The only way you can be successful in the markets is to develop a trading plan that suits your personality. It is up to you to lay the foundations yourself and develop your plan to blend with your lifestyle and personality.

In this chapter, **Justine Pollard**, a successful private trader and author, shared her thoughts on creating and documenting a trading plan.

Justine is a trader and author of *Smart Trading Plans*. Her book steers you through the process of developing and implementing your own personal trading plan to increase your chances of success in the market.

Visit <www.smarttrading.com.au> for more information and to download your free special report, *10 Tips to Smarter Trading*.

Get that monkey off my back

Mistake 4: not trusting your own ability

When I'm trusting and being myself ... everything in my life reflects this by falling into place easily, often miraculously.

Shakti Gawain

A key aspect to trading and investing is developing the ability to trust yourself and your own judgement of the market or markets you are trading. The use of a well-documented business plan and a proven 'system' is absolutely essential to your success. Success in any business requires entrepreneurs or business owners to thoroughly know and understand their business, their competitors and the overall business environment. Those who are consistent achievers, while prepared to listen to the opinions and ideas of others, have the strength of mind to implement their own twist on this information. Then they decisively and confidently make appropriate decisions for their business. The development of a well-researched and documented business plan is central to success. For traders, this written trading plan (as discussed in chapter 3) is well recognised as the first step to finding and maintaining success in any trading endeavour.

Despite the constant urgings for traders to develop, write down and commit to a trading plan, many still do not. They continue to place their faith in the judgement calls of other people—anyone from their supposedly well-informed brother-in-law (who also holds down a second job just to make ends meet), to the recommendations of an overpriced curve-fitted black box trading system that looks wonderful at the slick presentation night but fails to work in real time (see chapter 9). Why do people continue to ignore the fact that with the necessary preparation and some hard work they can develop the confidence to engage the market on their own terms and avoid the mistake of seeking the advice and opinions of other people?

Somebody else must know more than me!

Well-known Australian trader and educator Louise Bedford (<www.tradingsecrets.com.au>) offers the following view of why people ignore the need to develop their own skills and choose to defer the decision-making processes to others.

> Most people have honed a healthy respect for authority figures. In their past they have suffered consequences if they didn't listen to their parents or teachers, for example. Even as adults, we would like to believe that some people have the answers. We have an ingrained belief in expert authority, so if there is a newsletter or a broker that we can rely on to shortcut our painful process of learning, we will be very likely to trust in that source. Also, because most people are time poor, yet have a strong desire to discover a golden cash cow, it's just the simpler option to follow someone with perceived expert power. However, this is one area where you should probably make your own decisions and do your own research.
>
> Self-doubt runs rampant to epidemic proportions in our society. When you combine this with a task that is ambiguous and doesn't have a blatant right and wrong answer, the natural tendency for traders is to doubt themselves. One of the principles to consider in this arena is the concept of 'locus of control'. Our locus of control is an important determinant of success. An internal locus of control is the tendency to take responsibility for situations that are within your control to some extent.

An external locus of control is the tendency to believe that outside forces control everything.

Traders with an internal locus of control:

▷ usually have a realistic understanding of their own abilities

▷ know that they are completely responsible for their own actions

▷ do not rely predominantly on 'expert advice' (for example, a broker or newspapers)

▷ know that they cannot control the markets, only themselves

▷ react objectively.

Traders with an external locus of control:

▷ experience frequent self-doubt

▷ blame their broker or 'experts' when they make a loss

▷ have trouble learning from past experience because they do not take responsibility

▷ try to prove that they are 'right' rather than minimise their losses when a trade turns against them

▷ react emotionally.

When you become aware of your personal self-talk, it can help you to take responsibility for your own actions. It has the effect of helping you to learn salient trading lessons more quickly. The goal is not to identify yourself as a blind optimist. Some aspects of critical self-evaluation are desirable to trade successfully. For example, if you believe that it's not your fault that you continue to make losing trades, you may keep on trading until you have run out of money. Alternatively, if you seek self-improvement due to realistic, critical self-evaluation, this can greatly enhance your trading results.

Rather than aiming to become completely optimistic, stay true to your own character and become aware of your self-talk. Aim to learn when it is appropriate to take full responsibility, and when this method is counterproductive.

Three schooners and 1000 BHP shares, thanks mate

Trading of any sort is filled with emotion and, more often than not, huge doses of ego. So many people love to be the big shot at a dinner party or down at the pub on Friday night, telling anyone who will listen of their latest foray into a particular market and how they made a 'killing' in a particular trade. This, coupled with our innate human disposition to defer decision-making processes to others, leads to emotional involvement and attachment to trades. These trades are the ones where following some hot tip or piece of information, or reacting to a report in a newspaper or other media article, or a plain old 'gut feeling' that something is going to happen simply doesn't work out. Once in the trade, there is no knowledge of how to manage it and how to exit when it starts going pear-shaped.

Suffocated in a strangle

Here's an example of a trade Louise took that was influenced by her reading some fundamental information about a stock. The lesson here is how she reacted when the trade went against her and the lessons she was able to take from this experience.

> In April 1999 I performed a strangle on Newscorp, a particularly volatile stock (see figure 4.1). The share was in a flat trading band when a fundamental factor came into play. The stock took a massive Herculean leap right over my written call strike price of $13.00. (For those unfamiliar with option trades, this is precisely the thing your worst nightmare is made of when you have written a call option). Luckily, I had written puts underneath the share at $10.50 which provided a little consolation as these were now no longer at any risk.
>
> The strike price of my written calls had been penetrated by greater than the premium I received when I initially opened the position. I decided that a quick but graceful exit was essential. (Actually, it wasn't all that graceful and more resembled a knife fight in a phone booth.) I closed out the trade the next

day and took a nasty loss. However, the fact that I was out of the position let me sleep soundly that night. If I hadn't closed out at that stage, I would have dreaded each passing day of share price increase as my losses would have been mounting significantly. I faced a rather horrible loss, but it did show me that under pressure, I could mechanically follow my trading plan, and I could exit even when something completely unexpected occurred. The confidence that this provided me shows that you shouldn't judge whether you've made a good trade by whether you've made a profit or a loss. You should evaluate whether you're a good trader by whether you can follow your trading plan.

Ironically, the closing price of the share on the expiry day was less than my call strike. This would have meant that unless I was exercised early on the position, there is a good chance that I would have taken an unnecessary defensive action. However, I would rather jump out of a worrying trade than hold on and pray that my losses were not going to be catastrophic.

Figure 4.1: Newscorp share price, 1999

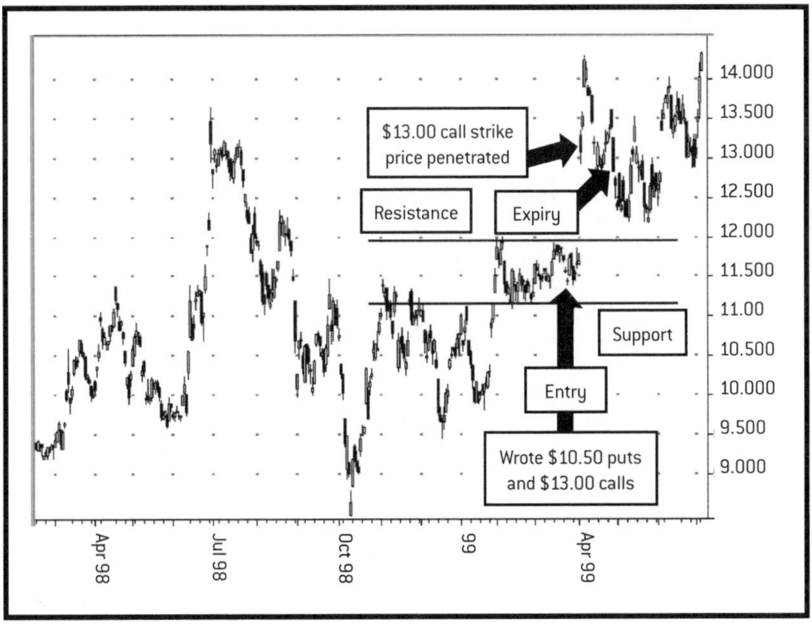

Source: © TradeStation Technologies, Inc.

Ah, sorry mate, you know that share tip? Well ...

Discretionary trading, where traders make decisions on the basis of non-objective rules, is a difficult and time-consuming process, littered with losses, frustrations and emotional turmoil. As the trader has no knowledge of why they really entered the trade — other than some hot gossip or a warm, fuzzy feeling — they have even less idea of how to manage and exit the trade. This adds up to losses piling up very quickly. The mate, broker or whoever else had all the hot news to enter the trade, has no idea what to do to get the hell out of the trade when it fails to work out. The short-term trade that was set to make a million bucks in the next three days now becomes a worthless long-term investment, or an expensive lesson in what not to do. Why, then, do so many people base their trading and/or investing decisions around these discretionary trades?

> The markets seem intent on teaching us bad trading habits. A core principle of the share market is that traders should let their profits run, and cut their losses. In effect, as a trade becomes more profitable, we should become risk-seeking and engage in strategies such as pyramiding. However, when a trade goes against us, we should be risk-averse, and the trade should be instantly exited.
>
> Unfortunately, the majority of traders have this rule around the wrong way. They become risk-seeking when faced with a loss, and they simply let it run. They are also likely to become risk-averse when a trade is profitable. The old wives tales of 'you'll never go broke taking a profit' or 'leave something on the table for the next person' come into play, and they exit the trade pre-emptively.
>
> It is difficult for traders to obey the rules of trading because their own psychology often defeats them. This concept is far more complex than it would first appear. Perhaps it comes down to the fact that these behaviours have been essentially hardwired into us by evolution. Much of human behaviour is merely a sophisticated replica of the sort of behaviours our ancestors displayed.

Imagine you are one of our primitive ancestors. The world is a frightening place. Virtually everything is bigger, faster and stronger than you are. The only advantage that you have is your ability to think ... but thinking is of little value in a life-or-death struggle. To survive this harsh environment requires a more robust, dynamic behaviour.

Suppose that you are out hunting in the primeval forest when, suddenly, a vicious predator leaps out from behind a tree and attacks. The only behaviour that will offer any survival advantage is to attack, and become risk-seeking. To run would only invite an attack from behind, as your predator is superior in speed.

This is the same behaviour that traders exhibit when faced with a growing loss. The evolutionary behaviour is to attack, to hold on to a trade, or to average down by buying more. In essence, we become risk-seeking. It does not matter that the trader is faced with a losing trade rather than a sabre tooth tiger. The behavioural response is the same. It is to become risk-seeking.

The same behaviour applies to the inability of traders to let profits run. Let's return to our primeval scene and imagine that this time you have come across a bounty. It may be a fruit tree or a fresh animal carcass. The instinctive behaviour is to grab as much you possibly can and then run. In this extraordinarily threatening environment there will always be something bigger, stronger and faster than you nearby. The caveman, like the trader, becomes risk-averse. While we may describe such behaviour in a variety of quaint euphemisms, it is still the same basic behaviour.

The world of our ancestors has also led to a variety of other behaviours that provide impediments to traders. In those ancient times, decisions had to be made rapidly, with limited cognitive input. Classification came before calculus. Is the movement in the bushes simply the wind, or is it something more sinister? The only thing that would ensure survival is a snap judgement. We have transferred this primitive level of thinking to trading.

The popular belief is that trading is a series of snap judgements and instant decisions made in the hostile environment of the market. This thought process also leads to statements such as 'BHP is a good share'; the implication is that good shares do the right thing. The right thing means they go up. Unfortunately, this is a primitive classification made by very primitive behaviour.

Trading is a precise and somewhat boring profession, where decisions are made long in advance of any contact with the market. The world's best traders realise this and they plan with meticulous care. Every contingency is considered and reconsidered. This approach may seem boring, and may not appeal to those who believe that trading should be frantically yelling 'buy' or 'sell' to your broker on a mobile phone while simultaneously admiring the upholstery on your new Porsche.

Another attribute that can lead to failure is the propensity for traders to listen to gossip and rumour. This is also an evolutionary behaviour. In primitive tribal communities, gossip was the only form of news communication. Those who understood this were able to secure a competitive advantage. This competitive advantage was likely to lead to greater breeding success. Hence, this behaviour was passed on from generation to generation. The desire to listen to gossip and rumour (or to search for the next big tip) is hardwired into us. We are programmed to respond to it. Yet, as traders, it is totally meaningless as a form of behaviour and effectively works against us.

In trading, our own evolution has conspired against us. The behaviours that in the past ensured our success, have in essence guaranteed that the majority of people will never make money through trading. The only way to overcome this is through self-awareness. Trading is not about 'feeling right'—it is about making money.

Quiet please, the movie is starting

The underlying principle is to develop a trading strategy that is as mechanical as possible to avoid the emotional turmoil of the market. The two main aspects of this trading strategy will be: developing your own skill base through education and learning *before* engaging the market (see chapter 2); and developing a level of self-awareness so that you are prepared emotionally and psychologically for the rigours of trading (discussed in this chapter). This will allow you to develop the confidence to trust both yourself and the system you have either developed yourself or been taught by someone with experience and knowledge of the markets. Commonly referred to as your 'edge' in trading, this is discussed in chapter 10. Mechanical trading systems are discussed in chapter 17. This ability to trust yourself and your system will allow you to engage the market and your trading activities with confidence and consistency. You will no longer need to listen to all the 'noise' of the market to make your trading decisions. Indeed, the aim should be to remove all this noise and outside influence from your trading decision-making processes, and simply trade according to the rules and structure you have developed for yourself.

Expert traders take responsibility and react objectively at all times. It is almost as if they do not have their own money invested in the market. They have developed a sense of detachment from their profit and loss results and, instead, aim only to trade well. They do not rely on the advice of others and tend to make their own decisions based on sound analysis. They definitely maintain an internal locus of control. Here are some of these qualities in more detail:

⋙ Wins and losses are indistinguishable in terms of their emotional state.

⋙ If the market does not 'behave', the expert trader takes impassive action to limit risk.

⋙ They analyse their winning and losing trades and learn from their experience.

⋙ They have a written list of back-tested trading rules and follow them without exception.

⋙ They trade to follow their rules and to trade well, rather than chasing profits.

Even if the lofty goal of detachment is not possible, the goal of self-awareness comes a close second. You need ample opportunities to learn about your own reactions to trading, and to plan in advance how you will respond to various situations. Nothing can stand in the way of the well-educated trader with market experience. Very few traders ever make such significant inroads into understanding their own psychology. For those who do, this will help set them apart from the average trader and provide a solid foundation for effective trading.

Louise Bedford is one of Australia's most compelling speakers on the sharemarket, as well as being a share trader for nearly 20 years. In this chapter she gave her tips on how to trust in your trading decisions.

Louise's trading books — *Trading Secrets, Charting Secrets, The Secret of Candlestick Charting* and *The Secret of Writing Options* — give practical, time-saving strategies that you need to implement in order to become an extremely successful trader. Louise personally trained me when I was starting out with my trading career, and I highly recommend that you check out her website <www.tradingsecrets.com.au>.

Nice knowing me

Mistake 5: not aligning your trading strengths

Any path is only a path, and there is no affront to oneself or to others in dropping it if that is what your heart tells you.

Carlos Castenada

Trading successfully and consistently requires a high level of diligence, application and hard work. Contrary to much of the literature and views of many 'experts', it is not a sure-fire way to riches with 'as little as one hour of work a day', or some other similar marketing catchcry. While these tag lines may appeal to people's dreams of raking in cash in return for very little work, the reality of trading is very different. There are literally hundreds if not thousands of hours of work required in learning, understanding and applying the skills required to be successful. This includes everything from learning technical analysis through to understanding market dynamics and a thorough knowledge and acceptance of who you are and how your personality will have an impact on your trading style and endeavours, and ultimately your success or otherwise as a trader.

Many individual traders and intending traders choose to ignore the fact that trading is a high-performance activity that requires a certain level of natural ability that can be enhanced through skills acquired and developed over time. Just as in sport, the arts, science and any other activity, some people will simply never make it. The majority of us will never play golf like Tiger Woods, paint like Picasso, surf like Kelly Slater or even cook like Jamie Oliver—we simply don't have the talent or skill set required to achieve what these people are able to achieve. They are 'naturally' good at their field and have developed and enhanced these skills through learning, improvement and application through hours and hours of practice and hard work. What we can do, however, is be aware of our limitations, recognise and accept these, and be totally honest with ourselves about our trading abilities and our ability to clearly define our 'edge'.

So you think you can ... sing?

Leading market-related psychologist and behavioural scientist Brett Steenbarger PhD has spent many hours with traders of all types, from individual long-term position traders placing one or two trades per week to those who trade tick charts on the equity index futures markets, such as the e-mini S&P, trading hundreds of times every day. He has seen and experienced a huge cross-section of traders and thus a huge cross-section of personality types. His views on the role of personality in trading are well established, as is his honest appraisal of personality as a determinant of trading success. Brett is also a trader. Unlike many market-related psychologists who don't trade their own money, Brett does. As a result he has a real understanding of the emotional demands of trading 'at the coalface'.

> Personality is a necessary element in trading success, but it is not sufficient to ensure success. Among individual traders, it is easier to believe that trading failures are due to psychological/ personality factors than to an absence of talent and skill. It is interesting, for example, to watch the season's opening episodes of the popular television show *American Idol*. Some of the contestants are breathtakingly awful in their singing. When given that feedback by the judges, however, they frequently attribute their shortcomings to nervousness. They don't want to face the reality that they lack skill, so they focus on situational

(and presumably modifiable) factors. Many traders are no different; they will chalk up their losses to lack of 'discipline' and refuse to examine whether their trading methods truly possess an edge in markets. The idea that a trader is going to pick up some chart patterns and indicator signals from seminars, books or websites and successfully compete with professional money managers who have access to reams of research, data and inside knowledge of money flows is no less delusional than the impulse that leads to those crazy Idol auditions.

In an ideal world, it wouldn't be necessary for me to emphasise such elementary realities. The retail trading industry, however, crucially depends upon the recruitment of new traders (as so many of the older ones fail). No brokerage firm, trading magazine, advisory service, seminar provider or coaching practice is going to get very far by emphasising the perils of trading, the talents and skills required for success, or the arduous process of cultivating those skills. As a result, the industry is complicit in sustaining the overconfidence and denial required for average people to believe that they can sustain a living from trading.

That rant aside, while personality cannot ensure trading success, it certainly can meaningfully contribute to trading failure. One constellation of traits that commonly contributes to trading problems, even among talented professionals, is an active, distractible, sensation-seeking temperament. This is most commonly found among people with attention deficits, but is common to risk takers overall. Traders with this temperament tend to seek action and stimulation and, as a result, rebel against risk management and prudent, rule-based, planned trading. Their impulsiveness leads them to make poor trading decisions, and this can lead to their demise.

People who have a tendency towards negative emotional experience — neuroticism, as it is called in the psychological literature — also have a hard time sustaining success in markets. Their anxieties, guilt and frustration interfere with clear decision making and lead to either undue risk-aversion or risk seeking. Stress is built into trading and its risk and uncertainty. It is difficult, however, to make money consistently when stress is experienced as distress. Very often that distress interferes with the motivation to sustain a learning curve and the resilience needed to weather expected periods of flat performance and loss.

These temperamental factors are trait-like; they are not easily modified. One implication is that there are people who are temperamentally unsuited for the risk and uncertainty of participation in financial markets. It is difficult to sustain a coaching practice by calling traders' attention to such simple realities, however, so this view is not commonly advanced in the trading literature. We can accept that not all people are temperamentally suited to be SWAT team members or research scientists, but somehow the notion that not all people are psychologically equipped to succeed at trading grates against our democratic instincts. We would like to believe that, with effort, all things are possible; that desire trumps talent. If that were true, I'd be in the basketball hall of fame by now.

Developing your skills

Having decided that trading is an activity that appeals to you and is one you wish to focus on and incorporate into your life plan, there are a number of steps necessary to develop and enhance the required skills. You need these skills to analyse the market or markets you want to trade, formulate trade ideas and then implement these consistently to achieve a profitable outcome. This learning phase requires study, reading, analysis, system development, understanding money management, and all the other key points covered throughout this book. There are also a number of positive steps that can be undertaken from a psychological perspective during this learning phase:

1. *Set reasonable goals.* To maintain a positive mindset and motivation, it is crucial that developing traders set themselves up for success, not failure and frustration.

2. *Set process goals.* It is useful to have goals related to profitability, but many of the best learning goals focus on the process of trading, such as keeping losing trades smaller than winners, sizing trades properly, and so on.

3. *Emphasise strengths as well as winners.* Your winning trades—and your profitable periods in markets—have as much to teach you as your losers. Indeed, it is probably more important to know what you do well, and make the most of it, than to waste time bringing weak areas up to average.

4. *Give it time.* Don't confuse a few weeks of success with favourable market conditions. Sustain your simulated learning curve across many market cycles, experiencing up and down markets and markets with low and high volatility. Take all the time you need to make your mistakes and to correct them.

5. *Keep a trading journal.* The journal is your way of structuring a learning process. It documents your goals and your progress in reaching those goals. It also helps you document your observations about markets and your self-observation. If you don't have the discipline to sustain a substantive trading journal, you probably won't have the persistence needed to make it through a learning curve.

Then, it requires practice, practice and more practice *before* engaging the market with your hard-earned dollars. Too many intending traders put their money at risk way too early and well before they have developed and refined these trading skills.

Simulation versus fantasy

The best way to achieve this practice is through the use of simulated trading. Simulated trading involves the use of a platform that relays real prices and real market movement and events ensuring you are making 'real' decisions to buy and sell, the only difference being that the trades aren't executed into the market. However, the processes of buying and selling, the emotional reactions, and the outcomes are quite real and expose you to the range of feelings, thoughts and outcomes that occur when really trading. Simulated trading also allows you to record and track the various performance measures such as profit/loss, win–loss ratios, and so on, that are vital to determining the success of your chosen trading strategy. This simulated trading effectively forces you to be totally honest with yourself about your ability to trade and with the overall effectiveness of the system being traded.

This is dramatically different from the paper trading or 'fantasy' trading employed by many when first attempting to test a trading strategy or their emotional involvement with the market. If not conducted in real time, trades can be entered or exited after the event, those that didn't 'work' can be avoided or left out of the equation, and various other aspects of the results can be 'fiddled with'. The end result is a less than true reflection of both the system and the trader's performance. This will have a very detrimental impact when the trader does attempt to then trade in real time.

> Because simulated trading takes much of the emotion around making and losing money out of the equation, it allows traders to simply focus on the process of trading. In simulated trading, traders can practise concrete skills, such as scaling into good trades or moving stop-loss points after a market has meaningfully moved in their direction. There is no fear of losing, and traders can make their mistakes without drawing down their capital. Only once a trader is successful in simulation mode should he or she begin to put real capital at risk by trading small size. If traders can't make money consistently without the pressure of a profit or loss, there's no reason to believe that they will be successful once the stresses of risk and uncertainty are added to the mix!

Add in a healthy dose of realism

> Yet another important psychological factor in the learning curve is the need for realism. Some traders begin with a small trading stake and dreams of making a living from their independent, full-time trading. That is not going to happen. Even the most successful portfolio managers are challenged to make consistent

returns of 25 per cent year after year without taking undue risk. If you start with an account of $50000, such a return will hardly make a living. If you place too much emphasis on making a living from such a small portfolio, you'll eventually take too much risk and lose everything. Your initial goal should simply be to learn good trading and to make money after trading costs (commissions, cost of equipment and software, and so on). Once you can sustain that, then you can address the need for additional capital either by saving up the money yourself or by trading a proprietary firm's capital. If your hope is to build a successful trading business, you need to have a realistic, attainable business plan. Hoping to double your money year after year without grievous drawdowns is not a plan. It's a fantasy.

Cheering for the team

Perceptual and emotional biases can have a negative impact on the outcome of individual trades and the success of traders. When a position is taken it is too often the case that the trader then looks for all the confirmatory evidence to support their view of the market while ignoring or minimising any evidence that is contrary to that view—these are known as confirmation biases and the 'endowment effect'. The trader then becomes attached to the position as they seek to be proven right in their analysis. Often this results in the all-too common mistake of holding on to losing trades and taking small profits on winning trades.

One way to combat these biases is to adopt the mindset of a scientist. Each trade idea is a hypothesis: we're expecting markets to move a particular way based upon our observations and experience. From this perspective, each trade is a test of our hypothesis. Like any good scientist, we need to define—in advance—what will constitute a successful and unsuccessful test of our ideas. In market terms, this means creating explicit price targets and stop-loss points for each trade or investment. The stop-loss point is that point of adverse movement that will tell us that we're wrong; that will disconfirm our hypothesis. By focusing on disconfirmation, we can avoid confirmation biases and endowment effects. Creating a plan for each trade that gives us greater upside (profit potential) than downside (potential loss) is an excellent way of staying grounded and objective after taking a position in markets.

When traders fail to plan, as the old adage goes, they might as well plan to fail. Without explicit trading rules that govern risk taking and concrete guidelines for taking losses and profits, traders and investors have little else to draw upon other than their feelings of the moment. These feelings commonly lead to biased decision making, in which hope can substitute for hard analysis.

Looking in the mirror

The ability to reflect on and observe both ourselves and our understanding of the markets from a distance is a crucial skill to develop. While at first this concept may seem confronting and a bit 'out there', it will allow you a greater insight into your interaction with the market, the way you trade, the time frame you trade and various other aspects of your engagement with the markets. Through observing yourself and your behaviour and reactions you will be able to refine and enhance your trading skills and your ability to deal with the huge range of challenges and issues the markets will throw at you.

One other psychological skill that is crucial to the developing trader is the capacity for observation. This includes self-observation and the observation of markets. Just as markets move in patterns of supply and demand, we have our own psychological patterns that are associated with good and bad trading. The ability to observe ourselves helps us formulate goals for our trading journals; the ability to observe markets helps us become more sensitive to repetitive trading patterns, so that we can act upon them in a timely way. Every losing trade, I believe, has the potential to teach us something. It may teach us about our mistakes, or it may teach us something about our market and how it is moving. If I place a break-out trade (anticipating a move above a trading range) and the market moves higher before reversing and moving back into its range, I've either learned something about my trade execution (perhaps I jumped the gun on the trade idea, not waiting for the break-out to be confirmed) or I've learned something about the market (there's not as much buying interest at a longer time frame as I had assumed). Frequently, a losing trade can teach us something both about our trading and about our market. It is not enough to view markets; we need to review them to learn from mistakes and to become more consistent in drawing upon our strengths. That is one reason the trading journal is important: it disciplines us to do the viewing and reviewing, day after day, structuring our learning process.

Aligning the planets

It is essential to ensure that your trading system or strategy is aligned with your trading strengths. Understanding yourself and your personality traits will determine what these strengths are. For example, you may find that your initial idea of short-term trading simply doesn't gel with your personality, lifestyle and goals. You may discover that despite all the reading and studying you have done, options trading simply doesn't make sense to you. The list of possible discoveries is endless. The important point is to be able to recognise and deal with these changes as they arise and make the necessary adjustments to your trading plan. This can only be achieved by fully knowing and understanding who you are, what you want to 'get' from the markets and trading, and how the two can combine to give you the best possible fit as a trader.

Many traders try to mimic the trading styles and methods of others, rather than develop the approaches that will work best for them. The result is underperformance and frustration. Many of the best baseball hitters and pitchers develop their own styles, and those styles often vary from what is commonly taught.

The key is to find the markets and methods that work for you, not to find a mythical Holy Grail that will work for everyone.

Where traders often fail to align their strengths and their trading styles is in the holding period of their positions. I tend to be quite risk-averse as a trader; a loss over time of several per cent will prompt me to cut my trading size and intensively review my markets and my trading. To stay within my risk parameters, I have to size my positions moderately and keep my holding times short. If I size positions too aggressively, I find it difficult to take even normal heat on trades. If I hold positions overnight, the increase in variability of my returns affects my subsequent trading. I am quite aware that this level of risk-aversion will prevent me from making large amounts of money in my trading. Indeed, because I do not trade for my living, my goal is simply to make more than the riskless rate of return (the return I could obtain from a Treasury bill or bank certificate of deposit) after costs. Trading is part of my deployment of capital as an investor, one in which I'm taking a moderate degree of risk to achieve a moderately enhanced rate of return. While that approach would not work for everyone, it fits my personality and my level of risk appetite quite well. When I've varied from that approach, usually by trying to hit trading home runs and extending my holding periods, the results have been dismal, and my trading has been personally unsatisfying. Trading intraday market swings in stock indexes is what I do best.

There are scalpers who trade much shorter time frames than I do, placing dozens if not hundreds of trades per day in comparison to my average of one or two. They not only watch every tick in the market, they also monitor the moment-to-moment shifts in the order book—and they do that through the day, every day. It takes a phenomenal level of concentration and commitment to sustain that trading. It also takes an unusual talent: the ability to process large amounts of information quickly. I lack that talent, and I do not have the level of concentration or commitment to sit in front of a screen all day, every day. It is the alignment of talents, skills and interests that enables the scalper to be successful. Most scalpers would fail miserably as longer time frame portfolio managers; just as many hedge fund managers would be lost trying to scalp each tick in markets.

The longer time frame investors and traders process their information explicitly, often as part of formal research, conversations with analysts, reading, and so on. They create explicit trading plans and hold regular reviews of positions and portfolios. As time frames shorten, more of that processing occurs rapidly and implicitly. The scalper who holds positions for less than a minute at a time has no time to formulate explicit trading plans. Rather, the planning is internalised as a set of guiding rules and parameters. The trader who excels at research and who enjoys formal analysis is more likely to succeed at the longer time frame.

We are most likely to stick with something and succeed with it if we enjoy it and find it to be personally fulfilling. This means that we need to discover and exercise our strengths, not trade in ways that are ill-suited to who we are.

Brett N Steenbarger PhD is Clinical Associate Professor of Psychiatry and Behavioral Sciences at SUNY Upstate Medical University in Syracuse, New York. In this chapter, Brett recommended techniques for aligning your trading style with your personality type.

Brett has authored several books on brief therapy and trading psychology. His latest work is *The Daily Trading Coach*. A trading coach at hedge funds, proprietary trading firms and investment banks, Brett writes the popular 'TraderFeed' blog <www.traderfeed.blogspot.com>, which covers market and trader psychology.

Easy come, easy go

Mistake 6: overcomplicating the entry process

O mischief, thou art swift to enter in the thoughts of desperate men.

William Shakespeare

Inconsistent traders are constantly searching for new entry rules, the latest whiz-bang indicator or fad and any new ideas that will supposedly help them trade 'better'. This search for the Holy Grail or perfect system is a time-consuming, soul-destroying act of futility that involves hours and hours of work and frustration until the trader finally realises that the perfect system doesn't exist. Much of this can be attributed to the fact that many 'educators', and dodgy trading systems sold by the snake-oil salesmen discussed in chapter 9, concentrate on the importance of entry signals when attempting to convince the unsuspecting buyer of the superior benefits of their trading system. These tend to place an over-reliance on entry signals as the be-all and end-all of a 'good' trading strategy. They are also great at showing plenty of examples of trades that worked perfectly based on this 'wonderful' entry strategy. Unfortunately, they have an uncanny ability to avoid discussing losing trades, the use of stop losses and money management techniques in general.

Many would-be traders are led to believe that entry signals are way more important than they really are. As a result, they spend time and energy in a constant search for the perfect entry signal, and continue to complicate the entry process—in some cases to the point where it becomes simply too complicated to use. This phenomenon is often referred to as 'paralysis by analysis'. Traders become so bogged down with indicators, patterns, strategies and formulas that they are unable to enter trades. They are waiting for so many of these things to line up perfectly before entering a trade that they never get to actually pull the trigger and enter the trade.

I'm not slow, I'm a turtle!

Renowned trader and educator Russell Sands is one of the original students taught by Richard Dennis in his legendary experiment showing that trading could be taught (referred to as the Turtle program). Here, Russell offers his views on this constant search for 'perfect' entry techniques.

It comes down to what makes most traders lose and not profitable: human nature and the need to be 'right'. Richard Dennis taught me as an Original Turtle Trader that we have to go against human nature. So, luckily, Turtles don't suffer as much from that problem. We use a straightforward 'breakout' entry technique, and cut losing trades quickly. Nothing fancy, just similar entry conditions applied with slightly different filters across a range of commodity and Forex markets.

Why do people think they need an edge or constantly search for something different? They assume that markets are different today from 80 years ago because of different execution speed, analysis techniques, information flows, and so on. But really, the factors of supply and demand never change much over time. Human fear, hope and greed—the basic Keynesian animal instincts were the same in the 16th-century Japanese rice markets as they are in the 2009 toxic-debt-laden markets.

In 1983 I was lucky enough to be taught how to trade a very simple trading method that, in its purest form, has only had one losing year since I was taught it. That's one losing year in 25 years, with 24, or 96 per cent, profitable years. That method averages 100 per cent per annum running at the position sizing I teach. In the 2008 full year that method made over 450 per cent trading commodities, while stocks lost 35 per cent!

That method is the Turtle trading method.

In short, what I am saying is that human nature wants new things and thinks they are getting an advantage. They are not. The Turtle method has not changed for 26 years and it still cranks.

We post our full trade results each and every trade since inception for the Turtle Forex program on the website <www.turtletrading.com>. Readers who are interested should look at that to see how it makes and loses money.

KISS this

Without doubt, the simple things in trading are, more often than not, the best. The markets are a complex mix of people with a complex mix of strategies that forge together to create a market of buyers and sellers. Where some see sell signals, others see buy signals and vice versa. The need to create complicated entry strategies adds further complexity to an already complex environment. Much of this stems from people's desire to attempt to control something over which they can have no control. The only variable in the market we can control is ourselves—our fear, greed and emotions, and how we interact with the market and adhere to our trading rules. The complex nature of the markets leads some to believe that in order to be successful they must have complicated entry rules that trigger trade entries only when several indicators and variables all line up at exactly the same time. However, this is far from the truth.

I don't really know why people think they have to over-complicate the entry process by using complex indicators and other technical mumbo jumbo. Maybe it makes them feel as if they are actually doing something!

KISS (keep it simple, stupid) works—the Turtles results prove it.

Seriously, human beings try to move from pain to pleasure. The average trader thinks if they optimise something away from the pain of past losses they will move towards profit (pleasure) in the future.

Over-optimisation does not help in the long run. The same trading concepts and parameters that Richard Dennis taught us Turtles in 1983 made me a lot of money in 2008. They have not been optimised.

Enter at your own risk

While entry signals are an important component of a trading plan, they need not be overcomplicated to the point where analysing entry requirements becomes the major focus. The 'best' trading systems provide clear and unambiguous entry (and exit) signals from just a few, often simple, criteria. Without entry rules we would have no way of knowing which markets and instruments to trade at any given time, but they need not be over-optimised in a futile attempt at perfection. The markets are an imperfect place; some trades will work, some won't—so what? Accepting this imperfection allows us to take the entry signals generated by our system. Coupled with an understanding of the probabilities of the system and applying strict money management and position sizing rules (see chapter 8), we are then able to execute the trades while always trading with stops in place to ensure we cut losing trades and profit from the trades that 'work'.

I have no idea as to why some traders seek to over-optimise entry techniques, other than human nature and the desire to seek perfection. Most traders scream and kick about slippage, but slippage is something I actually like in a trade—it proves the market is going my way.

I do know that I will make some very big trades every year and it does not matter what the price is when I get into those trades on the day of entry. I still will make a lot on those trades.

Cutting losses short is the most important factor—funnily enough it is what most losing traders use as a reason to object to Turtle Trading. Cutting losers means you clear out 'low expectation' trades and leave the better ones to grow and make us that little bit richer.

Trading is 20 per cent entry, 80 per cent trade and money management. Trade management includes a profit-maximising exit strategy.

As an example of this, an average winner in our futures and commodities system is entry at 100 per cent, out at 107 per cent after 28 days in the trade, and an average loser is entry at 100 per cent, out at 98 per cent after either two or nine days in the trade.

Running away from your ego

The need to be right is a function of our societal programming. Being 'right' is perceived as being smart. We are encouraged and rewarded for being right and for winning in all endeavours, from the sporting field to the business world. Trading is different. The need to be right is not rewarded as it is in other fields of endeavour. As mentioned by Davin Clarke in chapter 7, trading can reward you for being wrong. As long as you have appropriate risk management and money management rules in place, you can continue probing away at the market, taking small losses until the big winning trades come along and more than compensate for these small losing trades.

Trading also tends to reward simplicity over complexity. This point is mentioned by many of the traders in this book. The trading annals are filled with tales of highly educated boffins and others using complex mathematical algorithms and combinations of complicated indicators to achieve perfection in trading—on paper! However, when applied in real time, many of these end in disaster. The stellar implosion of Long Term Capital Management is one such example. It is almost amusing that the more complicated these 'systems' appear to be, the more highly educated the developers are, and the bigger the egos involved, the more likely they are to fail when applied in real time.

Our methods are simple and very profitable and they also are very, very effective. What our method does is surrender our ego to the process — we do not override our system and concepts.

Most people's egos are geared to being right. Turtles do not care about being right. We care about doing 'The Hard Thing', as Richard called it. 'The Hard Thing' is just following the system no matter how good or bad it feels.

The reality is that good trading does not take much effort. I have automated my order processing for myself and my customers so trading does not actually take up much of my time each day. That frees me up to teach and enjoy life and do whatever I want.

Maybe it's also a boredom factor — complexity satisfies our need to be seen as smart. I know a lot of very rich and not overly smart Turtle Forex traders who do not tweak anything; they just 'follow the rules'.

People have to get out of their own way. They have to have a system that is designed to work in many market conditions and stay out of the ones that are bad for the system. The Turtle method stays away from markets that do not meet certain trend conditions.

Making the shift

Having a simple and straightforward approach to trade entry shifts the focus away from the need to be right and towards a more thorough understanding of money management, risk management and the 'numbers' of the trading system or strategy.

It will also free up your time to explore other trading techniques and to spend less time poring over charts and analysis techniques. This can also result in psychological and physiological benefits.

Taking the emphasis off the need to be right all the time has the following benefits:

➲ Your psychology changes as you realise the more trades you take puts you closer to the long-run performance of the system you are trading.

> ⟫ Your physiology changes and you 'feel' better within yourself as you have become more empathetic with the market and your understanding of the game. Your ego is less important, stress levels are reduced and you can actually enjoy trading for what it is: a numbers game.

> ⟫ You end up just following the rules that have been proven to work in the long run.

Simplifying trade entry rules has many benefits. Not becoming preoccupied with complex interactions and the need for timing the perfect entry will ensure a massive shift in your trading psyche. Much of this revolves around accepting that you will be wrong and that being wrong is actually a good thing, provided you are adequately prepared. By accepting this you can get on with the business of trading and trade management rather than the search for the non-existent Holy Grail.

Russell Sands is a veteran futures and foreign currency trader who has been trading the markets for over 25 years. In this chapter, Russell shared his experience of success through keeping the entry process simple.

Russell learned how to trade in 1983 from legendary trader Richard Dennis in his famous trading 'experiment'. Richard's vision was to grow traders 'just like they grow turtles in Singapore'—Turtle Traders was born (<www.turtletrading.com>). Russell was one of the first 'Turtle' students taught trend following, specific rules, trading concepts and proven money management strategies. He has since trained a number of second-generation Turtles in Australia, Singapore, Japan, Malaysia and London. Russell holds an MBA from NYU and makes a living trading his own money, trading futures and Forex markets for other investors, and conducting educational trading seminars. He is also a Registered Commodity Trading Advisor (CTA) and an approved National Futures Association (NFA) Associate Member.

Complex complexity

Mistake 7: making trading too complicated

Simplicity is the ultimate sophistication.

Leonardo da Vinci

Traders can be easily bamboozled by the complexities of trading — hundreds of technical indicators, countless theories on how markets work and how best to trade them, and literally thousands of trading strategies and methods — complexity in a complex world. Add to this the urgings and offerings of many supposed trading educators intent on convincing the unwary that making money trading is easy — leaving traders totally confused and out of pocket when they realise it isn't — and it is easy to understand why there is an urge by many to overcomplicate the decision-making processes involved with trading.

Success in trading, as in any business or career path, requires lots of time and hard work to develop the skills necessary to engage the markets and profit from this interaction. With constantly changing market conditions these skills must be continually expanded and refined to ensure continued profitability. However, many traders and intending traders make the mistake of thinking that another new indicator, or the latest whiz-bang theory from some new 'guru' on the block will be their saviour and turn their poor trading results into thousands of dollars in profits by 5 pm next Friday. When they find this also fails, traders have now added another level of complexity to their trading repertoire.

Davin Clarke is an Australian-based trader. He trades short term moves on equities and indexes and uses derivatives to increase his exposure to dynamic and explosive short term moves. Davin shares his thoughts on why traders complicate virtually all aspects of trading.

> When you are told that something is easy, and then you discover that perhaps it is not so easy, it is a natural reaction to make it more complicated, hence verifying your experience. So, I believe one reason people overcomplicate the trading process is due to their prior experience with the market. Many traders feel the need to be 'right' and have the highest win rate possible. They cannot accept that trading is a numbers game and a proportion of losses are just a part of the process. I remember a presentation in 2006 where I started with the statement 'I had 4000 losing trades last year … I am the biggest loser in this room …' (at this point they were nodding their heads!) '… and if I had 4000 more I would have made twice as much!' The looks of shock and confusion on the faces of the audience clearly illustrated that they didn't have a grasp of the statistics. I love to actively day trade, looking for impulse moves with trades lasting from a few seconds, a few minutes or occasionally several hours. The result is I execute a lot of trades and my win rate is not particularly high; however, my edge ratio is high, so that the value of wins far exceeds the value of losses. If the statistics add up, you make money over time. It is completely unrealistic to expect to create a system that produces wins 100 per cent of the time. And yet, that is exactly what many traders are looking for. It is this constant search that sends them into analysis overdrive, searching for that elusive indicator or mix of indicators. The vast number and variety of analysis tools available can only result in creating a complex trading system.

The other reason people overcomplicate the trading process is fear. It is scary putting your hard-earned money at risk on the market. It is natural to want to ensure that you have everything 100 per cent right so that you won't lose your capital.

My system of trading is simple, as are many systems. The difficulty or complexity is in your ability to apply the system to the market. It is an art to be able to effectively read and 'feel' the market and apply your system to the market. It is also an art to read when you shouldn't. This skill is only developed through hours in front of the screen studying how the market moves and through experience of executing trades over time. Everyone can be an expert in hindsight—analysing past data and charts is no substitute for reading the market in real time. It is far more difficult to see set-ups in real time than after the fact. This in itself leads traders to believe there is something more they need to know. It is best to keep the trading analysis and process simple. This is not the only link to profitability. You must work on your skills in execution, understanding market dynamics and the market psychology that creates price patterns. It is this understanding of the market that is complicated and takes time and experience to develop. It doesn't require any particular qualification, but it does require an intense passion and interest in the market to devote your time to this pursuit.

Analysed but paralysed

The temptation to over-analyse market conditions often leads many to a point of absolute confusion, or to the point where they are waiting for so many indicators and conditions to line up in their favour that it becomes almost impossible for these conditions to occur. This results in the trader never actually getting around to the business of trading. They become so engrossed in the analysis of the markets that they never actually get to place the trade because they are, in effect, 'lost' in the world of analysis. They are able to show and discuss in great detail hundreds of examples of trades that 'would' have worked in the past and expound theories on what 'should' happen in the future when all the indicators line up. They can even talk about what they 'could' have done if only all their conditions had been met. Unfortunately though, they are unable to 'pull the trigger' and execute the trades as they unfold in real time. They become victims of the 'woulda, shoulda, coulda' mentality of many stuck in this world of over-analysis.

> Analysts are at risk of over-intellectualising trading to prove they are smarter than the market. These are the people who love analysing the market and creating great systems and indicators, but they are not traders. There is nothing wrong with analysts; in fact, they provide some great information for traders. However, there is a great divide between an analyst and a trader. I remember meeting a man at my trading club several years ago. He was so excited that he had found that elusive system that would revolutionise trading. He was in the process of writing his book on his system. When I asked what his returns were, I was a little taken aback to discover he hadn't put $1 on the market to test it!

Keeping it simple

The advice of many expert and professional traders and investors is to 'keep it simple' and not get stuck in this trap of over-analysing the markets and individual trades through the use of too many indicators and set-up conditions. But an important component of this process is researching and understanding both the markets you choose to trade and the 'tools' you will use to engage the markets in your trading operations. This is where the role of education and understanding becomes important. Study and learning is necessary to determine the techniques you will use to formulate the basis of your trading decisions and activities. It is wise to do this before engaging the market so you are fully aware of the workings of your chosen technique or system and its interaction with the market or markets you are trading.

> Keeping it simple doesn't mean that it is easy. By simple I mean using one or two trading strategies and ensuring you have clear

entry and exit strategies. For my personal trading, I find it better to focus on identifying a limited number of set-ups that provide a high probability of success with low-risk parameters. I have preset exit and stop-loss strategies for each set-up. Even though the process of trading itself is simple, it is the ability and skill to identify the set-ups in real time and being able to diligently apply your trading strategy while your money is at risk that is often far more difficult.

Technical indicators are, in essence, a combination of some factors of price and volume, and perhaps time. There are no other variables in the market that can be manipulated to produce a mathematical indicator. As a result, many indicators will give the same or similar entry conditions that may vary by a few minutes, days or hours depending on your trading time frame. Getting too hung up on the accuracy and specifics of these indicators and trying to determine the best fit for any particular market can waste a lot of time and effort. However, do the research to determine the indicators that resonate with your personality and trading style. Then determine, through further research, back-testing and chart analysis, whether or not they can be used to produce profitable trading results. The important issue is not to search for the one indicator or set of indicators that will produce profitable results 100 per cent of the time. None do! What is important is to know and understand the numbers: win–loss ratios, the size of winning trades versus losing trades, and so on.

The probability of success of your trading system and understanding your mathematical 'edge' is covered in chapter 10. It is this constant searching for tools that are accurate 100 per cent of the time that leads to frustration and confusion and prevents many analysts and would-be traders from actually pulling the trigger and really trading. They become obsessed with being right, rather than with studying themselves and the numbers and accepting that they will be wrong—in some cases quite often. If they know and understand their trading system and themselves adequately, they can deal with this and get on with the business of trading. The constant search for complexity and better entry techniques is a time-consuming exercise that is frustrating and without reward.

Trader development

The stages of development of traders or their level of experience and time in the market can be observed from their main area or subject of concern regarding the markets.

▷ New, inexperienced, fearful traders and those with a need to be right tend to be highly focused on entry techniques and finding the 'perfect' set of indicators or tools to make all their trades successful and profitable all of the time.

▷ Those with some experience and now less fearful of entering trades tend to be highly focused on exit techniques and endeavouring to milk as much profit as possible from each and every trade.

Experienced traders know and understand themselves and their systems well enough that their focus is on money management, risk management and order execution. They confidently go about the business of entering and exiting trades according to their predefined rules, knowing that they will profit from their activities if they remain in control of their money management.

I am a very high-volume trader. I have executed thousands of trades where the price action has moved as I have expected. I have also executed thousands of trades where the price action did not react as I expected. As I am very short term, with trades often lasting a minute or two, I don't tend to over-analyse situations as I don't have the time to. I have developed a keen understanding of how the market moves and how market psychology affects price through many, many hours watching and trading the market live. I am possibly more at fault of under-analysing the market. I base my trading strategies on my understanding of market psychology and like to read the price momentum as it is happening.

I have developed some longer term strategies (still intraday but looking for larger moves) that I consider simple in terms of the trading parameters. I have a predefined set-up that I look for based on price action and one additional indicator. The stop-loss and exit points are predefined. This 'simple' approach takes the emotion out of the trade and allows me to take full advantage of these high-probability set-ups.

Once the rules for engagement have been determined and you have a full understanding of your system, it is then vital that *all* the rules are documented in a written trading plan (see chapter 3). This will include the exact detail of your set-up rules, entry triggers, exits for losing trades (stop-loss), exits for winning trades, position sizing techniques, and so on. By working through this process of discovering the indicators and rules that work for you, you will have conquered the over-analysis monkey! You will have a simple and straightforward approach to the markets that is simple and suits *you*. From then on, it matters little what other traders, educators or friends think. You will know and understand what it is that you are doing and what you are trying to achieve. You will have a clear set of unambiguous rules that you know and understand and can use to execute trades with clarity and confidence.

> To avoid the mistake of over-analysing, traders need to overcome their fear of losing. This can include ensuring they are adequately educated, but more importantly have spent some time studying and watching the market itself to improve their understanding of how the market operates. Having a written and clear trading plan is another tool that allows traders to focus on the task at hand and not start looking for nuances and answers elsewhere. Starting small is also imperative. When new traders have too much at stake they tend to become emotional about their trading and lose sight of their trading plan.

Davin Clarke is a professional day trader who has been successfully trading full time for over 10 years. He started trading on the Australian equities markets and has now expanded his expertise to various derivatives, commodities and futures markets. In this chapter, Davin shared his views on why people overcomplicate the trading process.

Although Davin continues to trade the Australian market, his focus is on trading futures markets in Asia and Europe. Davin is a strong believer in continuous improvement and in adapting with the markets. He is always refining and developing new trading approaches and nuances to suit both his trading style and the markets he is trading. Davin often shares his knowledge with other traders through presentations at traders' clubs and the ATAA. You can learn more about his views and trading strategies from his blog at <www.trade4edge.com>.

Too many contracts, not enough shares

Mistake 8: not understanding money management

The safest way to double your money is to fold it over once and put it in your pocket.

Kin Hubbard

While traders the world over continually search for the 'perfect' entry system that will deliver them continually successful trades, those who have developed a portfolio or system-like mindset have come to understand and accept their 'edge' (see chapter 10). Understanding your edge also means knowing and understanding all the probabilities and range of outcomes that your trading system can produce — both negative and positive. This allows you to shift focus from entry and exit signals, to understanding the rules of money management. That is not to say that traders with good money management have given up the 'search', but they are able to continually research and test new entry and exit techniques knowing that, while the numbers and performance results of these 'systems' are important, it is the application of money management rules that will ultimately determine the outcome of any trading system or methodology.

One head, two hats

These traders are effectively able to wear two hats and separate their system development role from their role as a trader. The systems that they are trading are executed according to the rules they have developed and documented prior to any live or real time trading. This is their trading 'hat' — simply doing what they said they would, safe in the knowledge of the range of probable outcomes of the plan. The second hat — the system development hat — is the one they wear while developing and testing new ideas, concepts or trading systems. The two roles are kept distinctly separate so as not to cause any confusion and to prevent any 'thinking' occurring while they are trading. An integral component of their system development process is a thorough understanding of the money management model they will use. Specifically, we will refer to money management as the answer to the question of 'how many?' or 'how much?' of any share or futures contract we will trade.

It's simple, but it ain't sexy!

The vast majority of traders, investors, trading educators and trading-related media tend to avoid money management like it is the black plague. The focus for most seems to be everything but money management — entries, exits, new indicators, projections, forecasts, guesses, whiz-bang software all attract the punters like moths to a light. However, mention money management and people either ignore you, fall into a self-induced coma, or run off to mow the lawn with a pair of scissors if it means they will escape dealing with this vitally important issue.

Leading author, educator and trader Ryan Jones wrote *The Trading Game: playing by the numbers to make millions*, a book that explores the many aspects of money management in detail. Here, Ryan offers his take on why money management is often overlooked by the majority of market participants.

> In the trading industry, money management is simply not the sexy thing to spend your time or money on. Pick up any magazine and

a majority of the ads have to do with picking market direction, tops and bottoms, and things that deal with some sort of 'mystical market prowess'. It is my personal opinion that there is this idea that those who can accurately pick market direction possess some sort of genius that others don't possess. It is kind of an ego thing. Money management is not exciting. It is maths, and maths that virtually anyone can understand and apply. Consider this: over the past 20 years of being involved in this industry, I have talked with attorneys, doctors, engineers, rocket scientists, teachers, pastors—you name it—I have talked with someone associated with virtually every field of work except one...I have never once knowingly talked to an accountant who was also an active trader (not involved in this industry as an accountant). Generally, accountants are considered low-key, low-risk people from a personality standpoint. Let's be honest, accounting is inhumanely boring. Money management is boring, thus it just doesn't get the kind of attention like technical analysis and picking market direction.

Money management is simply not sexy. It is not promoted by people in the industry because it does not have the sex appeal to sell. It can be confusing at first. However, it really is not hard to understand for those who spend a little time with it. I also think it is ignored because there is ignorance as to how important it really is to the overall, long-term results. I believe that money management (or lack thereof) is the number one reason for failed trading attempts.

Thinking beyond the obvious

Traders are forced to add an extra layer of thinking to their plan when confronted with the issue of money management. Beyond the initial focus on searching for magical entry and exit techniques to deliver unobtainable returns lies the understanding of probabilities (see chapter 10) and recognising the importance of money management to the long-term success of a trading business.

Money management decisions are made every single time a trader enters the market, whether those decisions are conscious or not. Thus, from the beginning, no matter what you are trading, the money management decisions should be planned out before trading begins. Of course, there is room for changes to the plan as trading presses forward, but the major crux of the plan is in place. If you wait, you may miss the opportunity to capitalise on the profitable periods and this can be tremendously costly.

Money management is simple maths, but applying it to trading and a trading plan can be a little more complex. This is because the type of money management applied can have a dramatically different result on the same trading strategy and/or system. Money management is simply determining how much of your capital you are going to risk on each trade. This is done by determining the trade size. It is a decision that all traders must make every single time they enter the market, and whether they make it based on careful thought or little thought at all, everyone makes this decision. I try to encourage traders to make this decision before starting a trading strategy or system. Create a plan that clearly describes what your trade size will be at the beginning, and all details with regard to any changes in trade size. For example, if you start with one, when will you increase to two, or three, and so on? If you increase to two, three, four or whatever, what must happen for you to decrease back down to three, two and even one if circumstances warrant? These things should be determined prior to trading so that the trader knows what the ramifications are at each increase/decrease level. Generally, changes in trade size should be based on changes in equity and/or risks being taken.

The position sizing technique and the amount of capital you plan to risk on each trade *must* be incorporated into your overall trading plan, and *must* be documented prior to engaging the market. Properly applied money management techniques can greatly improve the overall performance of a successful trading system. In the event of the system or methodology entering a drawdown or period of poor returns, these techniques can actually prevent the system from completely 'blowing up' and losing vast amounts of either capital or accumulated profits.

It is estimated that 90 to 95 per cent of all traders fail (blow their account out) within two years. The very fact that so many traders risk their entire accounts (most don't realise this is what they are doing) speaks volumes to the importance of money management. On the flip side, proper money management can literally turn an average performing strategy into a multimillion-dollar machine in a matter of a few short years. How important is this? Consider the following scenario. Two traders trade the same exact system over the course of four years. The first three years are great. The fourth year the system falls apart and gives back a great deal of the gains achieved during the first three years. The trader applying a proper money management strategy would geometrically grow their account during the three good years and then protect those profits when the drawdown comes. The trader who does not is not efficient during the three profitable years, and ends up giving most profits back in the fourth year. The net result could be hundreds of thousands of dollars between the two traders.

Position sizing

Money management strategies help us to solve the 'how many?', 'how much?' questions, and to apply this strategy consistently in our trading business. Many traders and investors have little understanding of this concept. Despite hours of work and research devising entry and exit strategies, little (if any) thought is given to position size.

There really are only a few basic money management philo-sophies. For example, gamblers like to increase trade size after losing trades and/or after the equity decreases. By doing this, they increase the probability of making back losses with fewer winning bets. This is generally not for traders who have a positive expectation in their trading. It has been proven over and over again that the best type of money management when the expectation is positive (you expect to be profitable over time) is to increase trade size as the equity increases, not as it decreases. This is called anti-martingale (martingale increases trade size as equity decreases). There are several variations within the anti-martingale money management strategy. And there are some major differences in long-term results within these variations, which is really why it is so important for traders to understand money management in general.

Randomly choosing to buy or sell varying numbers of shares or futures contracts results in haphazard and inconsistent results. Worse still, traders often fall into the trap of increasing position size following a string of losing trades in an attempt to make back the losses they have incurred. This is a gambling mentality that will result in inconsistent results and ultimately will eventually destroy your trading account. This is known as a *martingale* money management approach — increasing trade size as the value of the account decreases. It is based on the ill-informed idea that the losing streak will eventually come to an end and the massive bet on the winning trade will make up all the losses and return the trader to profit. Unfortunately, it rarely works in real life. Consider the following example.

Example 1

Starting with trading capital of $100 000 and using the 2 per cent risk rule requires the trader to risk $2000 on the first trade. This trade is a loser, so the trader doubles the risk on the second trade to $4000, and it too is a loser. The third trade requires an $8000 risk and the third consecutive loss follows. The fourth trade now requires a risk of $16 000. The losing streak continues, requiring the trader to risk $32 000 on trade number five having already suffered losses of $30 000 from the first four trades. If this fifth trade were to lose, the account would be down by $62 000 and require the trader to risk $64 000 on the next trade. Clearly this is not possible as there is now only $38 000 left in the account.

Anti-martingale money management systems require position or trade size to decrease during a losing streak when your account size is decreasing, and increase as the account increases, thus causing geometric growth during these positive runs. They are the only type of money management systems that are employed by those with a professional approach to their trading business. Understanding and applying these strategies can have a dramatic impact on both the profitability and longevity of your trading business. There are five commonly accepted methods of anti-martingale money management strategies, as described here.

Equal dollar value model

Position size is arrived at by dividing the total available capital by the number of open positions traders believes they are capable of managing. It can result in huge variations depending on each person's belief in their capabilities. A share trader with a $100 000 account may believe they can effectively manage 10 open positions. Each position will thus have a face value of $10 000. Another may believe they can manage 15, giving a face value of $6600 to each position. Position size is then adjusted according to the value of the overall account as it rises and falls in value. The other major issue with this method is the huge variation in the price of shares. Dividing the capital equally between positions gives very small positions in high-priced shares, and massive positions in lowly priced shares. This leads to anomalies in individual trade risk and exposure.

When applied to the futures markets, this method manifests as trading one contract for every $x in the trader's account. Often, this is touted as $10 000. Traders with $100 000 would thus assume they would trade 10 contracts. If the account increases to $110 000 they would trade 11, and if it decreases to $90 000, nine would be traded. The problems arise when consideration is given to the positioning of stop-loss points, the differing contract specifications of individual commodity contracts, and the margin requirements of each contract. These are dramatically different between, for example, natural gas and corn. An initial stop-loss of, say, $2000 may be appropriate for corn, but would be ridiculously tight in natural gas.

Optimal F (fixed percentage) model

An extension of the fixed or equal dollar value model discussed above is using a fixed percentage of your total account for each trade.

Through back-testing and analysis the optimal percentage figure is arrived at and then used to calculate each position size. Optimal F is the optimum fixed fraction or percentage to place on any trade. If, for example, you determine that 15 per cent is the 'best' fit, you then allocate 15 per cent of your account to each and every trade. As the account grows, 15 per cent will be a larger dollar amount. If the account decreases, then 15 per cent of this reduced figure will be a smaller dollar amount. The major issue is that Optimal F calculations are based on the past and then applied going forward. You are effectively hoping that the Optimal F for the trades in the historic test period will be replicated in live trading now and into the future.

Percentage risk model

Using this method requires traders to define the percentage of total trading capital they are prepared to risk on each trade. Amounts from 0.5 per cent up to 5 per cent are often suggested. These will vary based on individual risk tolerances, trading styles and time frames. Using this model involves an arbitrary decision as to the size of the percentage risk to be used and the initial stop-loss level at which the trade will be exited—both factors that can hugely affect the results of each trade, as shown in the following example. This stop-loss level may be based on chart analysis, technical analysis or a randomly selected price at which the trade will be exited if it fails.

Example 2

Using $100 000 as available capital and applying a 2 per cent risk rule determines that $2000 will be put at risk on a trade.

Shares in XYZ are trading at $5.40, and a stop-loss level of $4.95 is arrived at from chart analysis, giving a loss per share of $0.45 in the event the trade is a loser.

Trade position size is calculated by dividing the $2000 risk by the potential loss per share.

$$\$2000 \div \$0.45 = 4444 \text{ shares}$$

However, if the initial stop-loss level is determined to be further away from the current price, say $4.65 or $0.75 per share, the resulting position size is smaller:

$2000 ÷ $0.75 = 2666 shares

If the same profit target exit price point is assumed, the larger position size will result in a much larger profit being realised.

The percentage risk model is a step towards varying position size in line with initial stop-loss values in combination with the maximum dollar amount that is to be put at risk on each trade. It also allows the percentage risk figure to rise and fall as total equity rises and falls. If the $100 000 used in the above example increases to $120 000, then the risk per trade will increase to $2400 ($120 000 × 2 per cent). If the account were to decrease to $90 000, then the risk per trade will be decreased to $1800 ($90 000 × 2 per cent). The shortcomings of this method are the subjective selection of the initial stop-loss points and the fact that no allowance is made for the volatility of the individual share or futures contract being traded.

Volatility-based model

The use of volatility takes the percentage risk model a step further and incorporates the fact that individual stocks and commodities have varying degrees of average price movements or volatility. This volatility is incorporated into the position sizing and money management model to more accurately reflect the effect these individual price behaviour patterns or 'personalities' can have. The net effect is that position sizes in instruments displaying high volatility are smaller than in those with lower volatility.

The major benefit of this method is that it dramatically reduces the amount of subjective decision making required to formulate the stop-loss point, and hence position size.

The most commonly used measure of volatility is *average true range (ATR)*. ATR is a measure of daily price ranges over a given period of time and can be used effectively in position sizing models. An ATR of $0.50 means that on any day, the instrument being traded is expected to move within a $0.50 range. This is its 'normal' price range. If we were to set a stop based on this value, it is highly probable that we would be stopped out of the trade on a daily basis. To avoid this, a multiplier of ATR is used to position stops outside of this normal daily price 'noise'. Various multipliers of ATR from 1.5 to 5 can be used, depending on the risk tolerance and individual needs and styles of traders.

This figure is then used in combination with the percentage risk model to determine position size. This allows position sizes appropriate to the volatility for every instrument to be calculated and applied to the trading system. Stop-loss levels can also be arrived at without any subjective appraisal, as shown in the following example. While this example has been taken from the commodity markets, it can just as easily be applied to share prices.

Example 3

Sugar futures are trading at 13.00 cents per pound and the 14-day ATR is 0.18 cents per pound. Each one-cent move in sugar equals $1120:

$$3 \times ATR = 0.54 \text{ cents per pound}$$

$$= \$604.80 \ (\$1120 \times 0.54 \text{ cents})$$

Stop-loss level = 13.00 - 0.54 = 12.46

Percentage risk: 2% × $100 000 = $2000

Position size: risk amount ($) ÷ 3 × ATR:

$$\$2000 \div \$604.80 = 3.30 = 3 \text{ contracts.}$$

If the volatility as measured by ATR was higher, the initial stop-loss would be set much wider and the number of contracts able to be traded would be reduced, as in the following example.

Example 4

Sugar futures are trading at 13.00 cents per pound and the 14-day ATR is 0.55 cents per pound.

$$3 \times ATR = 1.65 \text{ cents per pound}$$

$$= \$1848 \ (\$1120 \times 1.65)$$

Stop-loss level = 13.00 - 1.65 = 11.45

Percentage risk = 2% or $2000

$$\text{Position size} = \$2000 \div \$1848 = 1.08 = 1 \text{ contract.}$$

The shortcomings of this model are that stop-loss levels can have little relation to other potentially important price points. This may be just on key support and resistance areas, or in the middle of a previous day's price range. The stop-loss may need to be adjusted in these circumstances, resulting in redoing the calculations to ensure the position size remains within the risk parameters specified in your trading plan.

Fixed ratio model

This strategy allows the trader to increase and decrease the number of contracts or shares being traded based on the profits generated from a trading strategy or system. When a system is performing well, position size is increased and when it is suffering a drawdown position size is decreased, based on the profits or losses being experienced. It is suited to smaller accounts because it allows trade size to increase faster than in the standard money management systems which increase trade size slowly at first, and then more rapidly as the account size grows. These money management methods tend to favour increasing position size at the 'back-end', while fixed ratio increases position size much more quickly at the early stages or 'front-end' of a trading system.

Increases to the number of contracts traded (for share traders, a 'contract' can be a fixed number of shares, such as 500) occur based on a dollar amount of profit. This number is called the *delta*. It is arrived at by determining the largest drawdown previously experienced by the system and then using, in general, half of this figure as the delta. This amount can be varied depending on how aggressive or conservative you wish to be.

Trading a system that has experienced a worst historical drawdown of, say, $10000 would imply a delta of $5000. Applying fixed ratio to this system means that, after starting trading the system with one contract, a second contract can be added when the account accumulates profits of $5000—the total account size is $15000. Now trading two contracts, the trader needs to accumulate $10000 (delta of $5000 × 2 contracts) in additional profits before a third contract can be added—the total account size is $25000. The account needs to now reach $40000 before a fourth contract is added. (Accumulated profits of $25000 + $15000 from three contracts make $5000 profit each.)

A similar approach is used when decreasing contracts during a drawdown or following a series of losing trades. The delta applied can be varied so that decreases in trade size occur faster than increases to allow profits to be protected. From the above example, instead of waiting for the account to decrease by $5000 before trading one less contract, the trader may decide to use $2500. If the account drops in value by $2500, the trader then trades one less contract.

Decisions, decisions and more decisions

The choice as to which money management strategy to use will come down to personal preference, risk tolerances and a range of other variables. The most important decision is to actually choose one and implement it from the outset of your trading. Understanding and using money management is the key to success in a trading business. It will allow you to capitalise on the times when your trading system or methodology is working well and generating profits by increasing trade size accordingly. It will also ensure you protect both profits and capital during losing streaks and periods of drawdown by reducing position sizes accordingly.

Early in my trading career, I turned a $10 000 account into well over $21 000 in about three to four months. I did so by increasing my trade size and going on a fairly solid run. However, the money management I was using was one of the more popular fixed fractional strategies. Two weeks after hitting this equity high, my account dropped to only $2500! I was overtrading. I was implementing the wrong money management strategy for the risk I was taking. Back in 2000, I began trading a system and took a $15 000 account into over $107 000 in just three months. However, for the remaining nine months of that year, this system went into a drawdown and never came out. Had I not been using money management, the account would have ended the year at a break-even. However, because of the money management, this account ended up over 100 per cent for the year. I chose this example because it reflects the example of doing well for a short period of time, and taking advantage of that despite the system falling apart. The end result was still tremendously positive. I also use this example because I was being very aggressive during the drawdown. A more conservative approach during the drawdown could have preserved a return of well over 350 per cent on the year when the underlying system made virtually nothing without money management.

Understanding money management and risk management will move you from the realm of the uneducated punter to the educated trader. Knowing exactly 'how many' you will buy or sell when your trade entry triggers are confirmed shifts you to a new level of professional money and trade management. You will no longer be guessing and exposing yourself to positions sizes that are either too large or too small for your account size. You will also be able to clearly define when to increase and decrease your position sizes in line with your total equity.

Ryan Jones took his first trade when he was 16 … and lost. Being a super-competitive person, the 'challenge' was on. For the next five years, Ryan kept losing. There were many short-term successes, but they all ultimately ended in the red. At the age of 21, Ryan took six months off to analyse all of his trades and experiences. He made the startling discovery that would change forever how he approached trading — that money management is the key to long-term success. In this chapter, Ryan explained the importance of this discovery.

Ryan has recorded many impressive trading feats, and in his 22-year trading career has traded nearly every major market using a vast number of trading strategies. Ryan has developed over 1000 technical analysis-based systems and created advanced trading courses. He is the author of *The Trading Game: playing by the numbers to make millions*. Ryan is currently creating the most advanced technical analysis and system development software program to hit the industry: <www.smarttrading.com>.

1000 per cent return in three days — sure, it happens all the time

Mistake 9: paying good money for a dodgy trading 'system'

The public will believe anything, so long as it is not founded on truth.

Edith Sitwell

We've all seen and heard them at trader expos, seen the glossy ads in the papers and magazines, and received their flash emails with glowing reports and testimonials. We've all been tempted by the promises of hundreds of per cent returns on our initial capital for doing nothing other than sitting back and watching the cash magically roll in from the new wonder trading system or indicator that will churn out the signals and make us filthy rich within the next three weeks while we watch TV or sleep.

Alas, while the vast majority who are targeted treat this rubbish with the contempt it deserves, some suckers actually fall for the charms and sales pitch of these snake-oil salespeople. They are drawn to the promises of riches and greatness with flashy scenes of fancy cars and deserted tropical islands, wads of cash, and arms full of gold and jewellery. Little do they realise that the only ones driving the fancy cars and sailing off into the sunset are the salespeople and promoters of these empty schemes and dodgy trading systems.

The unsuspecting purchaser, who has parted with his or her hard-earned dollars, is left with little more than a series of bad trades, money losses, and a bitter taste in the mouth. Yet people are continually drawn to these 'systems' in the hope of making a fast buck from the market with little or no preparation, understanding or hard work.

Learning to play the piano

Wayne McDonell from Fx Bootcamp (<www.fxbootcamp.com>) has been trading in derivatives and Forex for over 20 years. As a presenter and educator of both Forex and futures traders, Wayne has seen and heard the marketing ploys and pitches of the 'snake-oil salesmen' thousands of times. He has his views on how and why people continually fall for these dreams of magical returns—usually people who cannot afford to lose any more money.

> There are literally hundreds, if not thousands, of so-called systems selling what I like to call 'green arrow and red arrow nonsense'. One must never underestimate the power of dumb money and people's desperate situations that draw them to the promise of making easy money. The current global economic crisis has heightened this level of desperation, but it usually exists among a certain group of people most of the time anyway. These are people for whom an existing investment or trading methodology has turned sour, resulting in them incurring losses and seeing their wealth reduced. Some of these people who are heavily invested in stocks in their retirement plans or superannuation funds have seen their 'nest eggs' and portfolios drop by up to 50 per cent, and in some cases even more over the past year or so. This effectively means they will have to keep working for another 10 or 20 years before they can retire. These people get desperate. They are looking for something to help them recover from this catastrophe, and as such are lured to these promises of easy money like moths to a light. Their mindset is that they have to do something, and they have to do it now! They decide to take $10 000 from their retirement

fund, which is losing value anyway, and have a 'punt' on this wonderful new system that promises to make them back all the money they have lost, and then millions more in the process while they lie on the lounge and eat potato chips. However, there is a huge disconnect between what they need and the reality of how to get it. Achieving the sort of success and profit promised by these promoters is like waking up one morning and deciding to become a concert pianist within the next six weeks or your life is doomed — it's not going to happen. It is impossible to become professional at anything within that time frame. No piece of software, fantastic new indicator, or DVD box set is going to teach you how to trade or play the piano like a professional. It takes years and years of dedication, practice and hard work — 'blood, sweat and tears for years'. This is the only path to long-term success in trading.

There are always new waves of suckers and desperate, ill-informed people drawn to the world of trading. They either want or need to do something but they don't know what 'it' is. They continue to fall into the same old traps over and over again. They are looking for hope, a dream or an easy option. They aren't prepared to face the reality that trading requires hard work and perseverance to be successful. So, they take the easy options offered by these promoters and vendors and invariably it costs them time and money that they couldn't really afford to lose in the first place.

These outrageous claims of easy money from curve-fitted systems, where the data has been manipulated to produce fantastic results, usually display a snapshot of a small data sample that the promoter extracts to convince the unsuspecting purchaser of the profitability of the system. The system vendor displays a small period in which the system performed exceptionally well. What isn't shown is the next period, over a much larger data sample, where the results of the system were far from impressive, or even worse, actually lost money. The promises of making a quick buck with little or no work and the intrigue of both the markets and the trading environment combine to draw people in and help them part with their hard-earned cash. Like a fish drawn to a lure, they are reeled in, convinced with some slick selling that the system will solve all their financial woes, parted from their cash, and spat out as the proud owners of a dubious trading system.

> These people are desperate to make money, recover losses or escape their dead-end, cube-farm job with petty office politics and a three-hour commute. They are fed up with it, and are willing to do just about anything to get out of their current environment. They want something better for themselves, to break down the walls and get out of the 'rat race', to become their own boss. Their entrepreneurial spirit draws them to the idea of trading — of buying and selling commodities, shares or foreign exchange. It's also the appeal of a business with no staff, no inventories, no debtors and creditors and the potential for huge returns if the required skills can be mastered. The snake-oil salespeople play to these emotions. They are well aware that these people are in the market for something that will launch them into a successful trading business with little or no work. They prey on their entrepreneurial spirit and their desperation. The vast majority of retail traders are hungry for something that will change both their financial and personal situations. There is a huge market of naive and unsuspecting potential clients for these sharks to prey on — selling software and dreams to feed their hopes and quell their feelings of desperation.

A reality check

If trading were really as simple as buying a magical trading system from someone else, plugging it into your computer and then sitting back watching the profits roll in while you got on with all the fun things in life, why isn't everyone simply doing this? Why are people going off to work in meaningless jobs that crush their spirit and consume most of their lives, when they could all be sailing around the tropics in their yacht, along with the rest of the world? If the claims of the people marketing these wonderful systems were to be believed, there would be no-one left in the world to do anything, as we would all be too busy lazing around doing nothing other than thinking up ways to keep spending all the cash that was pouring into our bank accounts from these truly amazing trading systems.

Can a magical system that you simply turn on really work? A secret, magic, voodoo system that looks at 7000 indicators and then combines it with some fuzzy logic that only a computer with its super high-powered analytical capabilities can perform in the nanosecond required before the market changes again? It isn't reality. It doesn't matter if these people claim to have a mother spaceship beaming the information to them, or if the CEO of the company can travel through time, find out what happens in the future, and then come back and tell the system what to buy and sell and when — it's all rubbish.

Think about it logically. If you could turn one of these systems on and have it trade away for you 24 hours a day, 7 days a week, 52 weeks a year, for years and years, you would make millions of dollars — if it worked. As the account continued to grow and with the use of leverage, your position sizes would be enormous. And so would everyone else's. Can the markets really absorb all this volume? Can everyone just buy one of these systems and watch as their accounts grow and grow? Who would you be trading against? Honestly, if the system or indicator or special magical formula is as good as the claims they make, why are they at an expo trying to sell it to you for a few grand, and not sitting on their yacht in some tropical paradise living the dream they are promoting? Because it's all rubbish.

It's not a serious plan to even consider putting your hard-earned money into one of these scams. When it fails and you lose your money, do you really want to be 72 years old and still working at a coffee shop stealing muffins when the manager isn't looking? A sane person wouldn't believe any of this hype and slick promotional material. Sadly, though, people aren't always sane when it comes to trading. They are hungry for quick success, desperate, emotional, and they need a way out. They want a better life and a better future and they are tempted into taking what appears to be the fastest path to make their fortune and live the life they have dreamed of.

Doing what it takes

Building a successful trading business doesn't revolve around buying a dream or being sucked in by the hype of the myriad dubious trading systems touted by these slick salespeople. While having a burning desire and the entrepreneurial spirit to be attracted to trading is a great first step, searching for the easy answers and a magical trading system, and parting with a large chunk of your start-up capital to purchase it, is definitely not the way to go. As with building any business, it takes hard work, commitment and a willingness to learn. Relying on a decision-making process that you do not understand, and the signals provided by a 'magical' black box trading system is effectively trading suicide, and is akin to playing financial Russian roulette.

> These systems are rubbish! If you have to rely on any magical indicator or black box system that isn't fully disclosed and explained, it's financial heresy. Astral cycles, planetary align-ments, secret codes and formulas, mystery indicators—it's all a hoax. The only way to build a successful trading business is to learn the necessary skills yourself and then become proficient and professional in the application of these skills. There are three critical skill areas that need to be learned and understood:
>
> ▷ Most importantly, learn technical analysis. If you are an investor who buys stocks and leaves them in the drawer for 25 years, then you don't need to waste any time learning technical analysis. Investors don't necessarily look for an exit. They are after growth and long-term asset appreciation—a strategy that has been blown out of the water in recent times. If you are a trader, or want to be a trader—trading anything from tick charts up to a few weeks or maybe months—then you must learn technical analysis. You must be able to clearly define legitimate entry and, most importantly, exit signals if you want to speculate and make money. Technical analysis skills tell you when to press the button to enter and exit trades. There are many different types of technical

analysis and you will have to do the research and work to determine the type that suits you and your trading style. It all works, and it's all appropriate as long as you understand it and apply it with consistency and discipline.

⇨ Once you have a sound foundation in technical analysis, learn the basics of fundamental analysis. Technical analysis will get you into and out of trades but may not tell you why trades present themselves or why a market is moving in a particular direction. Fundamentals are the initial drivers of any trend and represent a global money flow from country to country, commodity to commodity, or currency to currency. A prime example is money flowing into Australia to purchase natural resource commodities and to invest in the companies associated with this industry. The biggest fundamental driver is inflation and how the central banks of each country deal with this inflation — are they raising interest rates, lowering interest rates, or are they paused? This simple notion of interest rates and central banking policy towards interest rates is what fuels long-term trends in commodity and currency markets. Unfortunately, the majority of traders give themselves too little time to learn. They jump into the market with both feet after buying a DVD or some crazy black box trading system, put 10 grand into an account, burn through that, and are then out of the market. If you learn and master technical analysis, and then spend time learning macroeconomics and understanding the major economic indicators, you will understand why valuations of any financial instrument change, why trends begin, and how to trade these trends.

⇨ You must learn how to *be* a trader. Learn how to master your emotions and how to manage your trading business — how to manage risk and your budget, how to think in terms of probabilities. These are the solid trading habits that all traders need to have if they are to be successful. You can't get this from a 'magical system' or DVD that you pick up from a conference, expo, trading magazine or the internet. These are skills that have to be learnt from another human being. It's a person-to-person interaction and a transfer of knowledge thing.

Sorting the wheat from the chaff

Building a successful trading business takes time, patience and hard work. It can't be achieved in an instant by purchasing an off-the-shelf black box system with limited knowledge of how it really works, and that promises to deliver you millions of dollars in return for little or no work on your part.

There are many trading systems and strategies that do work. These are built on solid foundations and sound logic that includes well-defined entry and exit rules, and logical risk management and money management strategies. These systems will usually be 'low-key' and able to display realistic levels of returns across a large data sample over many years of real-time trading. Extensive learning and education components may also be associated with the system. The aim is to teach people how to understand the workings of the system, and thus to advance their learning and become better traders. The good system developers and vendors are open and honest with their results and are able to discuss and demonstrate a wide range of both winning and losing trades. While they may contain a proprietary indicator or function designed to give the system its 'edge' in the market, they won't be built around magical indicators, secret formulas and other mumbo jumbo. They will usually adopt a quite simple and straightforward approach rather than an overcomplicated multitude of bizarre interactions.

These guys will also be happy to discuss with you all the statistics and numbers associated with the system and its results. They will happily disclose winning and losing percentages, win–loss ratios, payout ratios, drawdowns, winning and losing streaks, and any other information you care to request. Essentially, they have nothing to hide, and are only too willing to discuss these numbers with you to display the robust nature of the system over a range of market conditions. If you intend to trade a system in this way it is imperative to adhere to the rules of the system with consistency and discipline and to take every signal generated by the system. It is a big mistake to attempt to 'cherry pick' the best trades, or to turn the system on and off outside the guidelines or signals generated by the system. Only by adhering completely to the rules of the system can you hope to replicate its performance and thus generate the returns available.

Wayne McDonell is the Chief Currency Coach at FX Bootcamp (<www.fxbootcamp.com>), a live Forex training organisation that teaches traders how to develop conservative trade plans based on technical and fundamental analysis, as well as addressing the psychological aspects of being a trader, in real time 12 hours per day. In this chapter, Wayne exposed the truth about trading systems.

Wayne is a popular speaker at Forex conferences around the world. His online Forex training videos are syndicated by <FXstreet.com>, <DailyFX.com>, <MSN.com> and Yahoo Finance, among others. He is a regular media contributor on currency trading. Each Monday, Wayne is the featured guest on Forex Television's 'PM Exchange' and he writes a monthly Forex column, 'Currency Corner', in *YourTradingEdge* magazine (distributed throughout Australia and the United Kingdom). Wayne has written 'how to' articles for *The Forex Journal, Traders Journal, Currency Trader* and *Futures Magazine*. Wayne's book, *The FX Bootcamp Guide to Strategic and Tactical Forex Trading,* is highly acclaimed and a best seller in the 'foreign exchange' category of Amazon. FX Bootcamp is a member of the National Futures Association and registered as a Commodities Trading Advisor.

Heads, I win; tails, you lose!

Mistake 10: failing to understand the numbers

The 50–50–90 rule: anytime you have a 50/50 chance of getting something right, there's a 90 per cent probability you'll get it wrong.

Andy Rooney

Accepting that trading is as much about losing as it is about winning is a dramatic leap forward for any trader. This is a sure sign that a degree of professionalism and acceptance of the fact that not all trades will be winners has been achieved. From an initial focus on the need to nail down the 'best' entry technique, progressing to a focus on clearly defining an exit strategy, the final phase is the realisation that money management skills (see chapter 8) are the most important aspect of any trading business.

Associated with this is a clear understanding of all the numbers involved with any trading system and understanding your mathematical 'edge' in the market. This acceptance of losing and being able to deal with the loss in a clinical and businesslike fashion is achieved through both personal development and acceptance, and also through a complete understanding of the range of probabilities and outcomes of the system being traded or the approach being used to engage the market.

You loser!

To reach a state of acceptance, first must come the realisation that, despite all our conditioning to the contrary in other areas of life, losing is actually okay in a trading business. Early in life we are taught to believe that losing is bad, and that to be successful we must be a winner. This conditioning applies throughout school, business, sport and even the social environments in which we participate. We are constantly encouraged to compete to win, and winners are praised for their achievements. Losing is treated with disdain and we suffer the negative emotions of anger, disappointment and frustration when we lose. We think we have failed when we lose and we worry that society and our peers will judge us as losers. These negative emotional reactions to losing trades create frustrations and can cause the unwary or uneducated trader to begin erratic, unwarranted and subjective decision making which creates more disappointment, poor results and dwindling capital. Successful trading is the opposite.

Losing is the new winning

The weird anomaly in a trading business is the fact that the more you lose, the more you win as long as your system has a proven probability of success over a large data sample. That is, by continually applying a proven system and constantly probing the market for opportunities, one will be continually dashed by dodgy leads and trades that go nowhere. The trick is to keep these losses to a minimum through the use of stop losses and risk management techniques and then to take full advantage of the winning trades when they do come along. Only in this way can profitable trades be uncovered. If we aren't continually searching for potential opportunities and entering trades according to our rules, then we have zero chance of success.

We cannot hope to participate in winning trades by waiting in the wings. This will only lead to further frustration as the winning trades leave us watching from the sidelines wishing we were involved, but knowing we didn't have the guts to enter the trade because we didn't initially want to get it wrong! We need to develop absolute trust in the system we are trading so that entry, exit and all other rules are followed judiciously and without any need to second-guess or override the signals. This can only be achieved if we fully understand the 'numbers' that give us this edge. Successful traders think in terms of probabilities—not in terms of winning and losing—on each and every trade.

Gary Stone, managing director of Sharefinder and developer of the SPA3 Share trading program, shares his insights here.

> People in this position (of concentrating on individual trade results) are different from a skilled trader who looks at the market objectively and empathetically. Both have experienced the same conditioning from their environments. However, skilled traders have learned to think, feel, see and act differently.
>
> Winning, losing, new portfolio equity highs and portfolio drawdown are seen by the skilled traders as the probabilities playing themselves out in the market. These are normal occurrences for the skilled trader; in fact, he or she expects them to happen.
>
> To make the transition from a novice trader's perspective to that of a skilled trader who is empathetic with the market, means changing ingrained beliefs and reprogramming our mindset to a new way of thinking—thinking in terms of these probabilities.

Empathy

The Macquarie Dictionary defines empathy as 'mentally entering into the feeling or spirit of a person or thing; appreciative perception or understanding'. In trading, having empathy with the market means you move from a focus on being right and measuring each trade as a winner or a loser to accepting the outcome of each trade regardless of the result and measuring your overall performance based on the probabilities of the range of outcomes over time.

> These probabilities are determined by the number of times that you win and how much you win compared with how much you lose, on average, over a large sample.
>
> When this is measured through research over a large sample of trading events, through different types of markets, you can

determine the mathematical expectation for the way that you trade. More on mathematical expectation below. If you cannot understand or define your probability of success, then you are gambling and should not commence trading until you fully understand your probabilities of success.

Many novice traders draw rash, subjective and impulsive conclusions from small samples and brief experience. Immediate success is craved, if only for building confidence and self-determination. This is another trait learned from modern society: instant rather than delayed gratification. It is normal to want to win as many times as possible, especially early in a new enterprise. The confidence gained from success in a small sample leads to an expectation of future success. However, sophisticated traders define their edge precisely, know the probability of success that it represents, know the term over which it delivers success, and know that an adequate sample size is required for long-term results.

Most traders do not understand or fully accept this concept. Many dismiss it as unimportant — but most of these traders are destined to failure. I suggest that being empathetic with the market is an absolutely essential component in the make-up of every successful trader.

So, you're expecting...

A major key to success is understanding the mathematical expectation of your trading system or methodology. This is referred to as your 'edge'.

Mathematical expectation, or expectancy, is what you expect to win or lose, on average, for each trade over a large sample of trades. It is essentially a benchmark number that tells you whether you have an edge or not. If the mathematical expectation of your trading approach is a positive number, then you will achieve a positive outcome if you trade according to the system's rules, which are based on the probability of winning and on the size of the winnings compared to the size of the losses.

As wins and losses come from the market, you need to think in terms of the probabilities that are achieved from the way you trade and the time frame in which you trade. The way that you trade is your system, defined by entry and exit criteria and the amount of capital that you allocate to each trade. Your system should, therefore, be extremely well-researched with unambiguous criteria that define the signals, and have a positive expectancy.

Crunching the numbers

To understand mathematical expectation, let's consider the example of tossing coins. The probability of correctly calling a head or a tail from one coin tossed is 50 per cent, or 0.5. In a game with one coin, if I win $1 when I call heads or tails correctly, and lose $1 when I call incorrectly, I would expect to break even because a single coin will only produce a head or a tail, and tossed many times it will produce the same number of heads as tails. The *mathematical expectation* of this game is break-even. This is represented mathematically using the following formula:

$$ME = [1 + (W/L)] \times P - 1$$
$$= [1 + (\$1/\$1)] \times 0.5 - 1$$
$$= 2 \times 0.5 - 1$$
$$= 0$$

Where:

ME = mathematical expectancy

W = amount you can win; L = amount you can lose

P = probability of winning.

A mathematical expectation of zero means that you will neither win nor lose money—that is, you will break even.

It is obvious that for 10 consecutive coin tosses, if we win five and lose five and we win $1 when we win and lose $1 when we lose, we will end up breaking even. However, if we win six times and lose four times, we will profit by a total of $2. Our six winning trades have returned a total of $6.00, while our four losing trades have cost us $4.00, so our profit is $2.00.

Say we had a way of consistently doing this—winning an average of six out of every 10 coin tosses, or 60 out of 100, or 600 out of 1000. That is a probability of winning of 60 per cent (P = 0.6), and we still win and lose $1.00 on each coin toss. Let's represent this as a mathematical expectation:

$$ME = [1 + (\$1/\$1)] \times 0.6 - 1$$
$$= 2 \times 0.6 - 1$$
$$= 0.2$$

Being greater than zero, this is a positive mathematical expectation and means that you have an edge and you can make money. Alternatively, suppose that you won five out of every 10 coin tosses (P = 0.5), but your winning calls attracted a win of $1.10 and your losing calls a loss of $1.00. The mathematical expectation of such an edge is:

$$ME = [1 + (\$1.10/\$1)] \times 0.5 - 1$$
$$= 2.10 \times 0.5 - 1$$
$$= 0.05$$

While this is a smaller amount than the above example, it is still a mathematical edge.

Both of these 'edges' will result in a positive outcome after a large enough sample of coin tosses. Regardless of the outcome of each individual toss of the coin, we can play knowing that, over time, we will be profitable. We are now focusing on the long-term probabilities of the 'system' rather than the outcome of each toss of the coin.

An example of a negative mathematical expectation is one where a win pays $1 and a loss incurs a loss of $1.10:

$$ME = [1 + (\$1/\$1.10)] \times 0.5 - 1$$
$$= 1.91 \times 0.5 - 1$$
$$= -0.096$$

In this negative edge example, where our chance of either winning or losing is 50 per cent (P = 0.5), we eventually lose all our capital if we continue to execute all possible events. Obviously, we do not want to trade a system or methodology that has a negative expectancy.

The two linked factors that determine your mathematical expectation are:

▷ how often you call correctly (win) versus how often you call incorrectly (lose)—your probability of winning, and

▷ the average amount you win when you call correctly versus the average amount you lose when you call incorrectly.

Knowing these numbers allows you to determine whether you have a positive mathematical expectation—an 'edge'—in your trading business.

Let's look at a simple example of a trading system with a positive mathematical expectancy or 'edge'. This example shows you how to work through these numbers with your own results to determine your edge. From accurately kept records (see chapter 20) we are able to arrive at the following statistics for this theoretical system.

Number of trades = 1000

Total winning trades = 610

Total losing trades = 390

Probability of winning (P) = 0.61

Size of average win (W) = $1150 (including brokerage costs)

Size of average loss (L) = $640 (including brokerage costs)

$$ME = [1 + (W/L)] \times P - 1$$
$$= 1 + [(1150/640)] \times 0.61 - 1$$
$$= 2.80 \times 0.61 - 1$$
$$= 1.72 - 1$$
$$= 0.72$$

It is important to calculate the size of your average win and average loss after the inclusion of brokerage costs. Brokerage costs will vary depending on a number of issues and can have a massive impact on the long-term outcomes of trading performance. If we were to calculate the expectancy of the system in the example above and not include brokerage costs, the result would be significantly different.

Overleaf I have used brokerage figures of $80 per side ($160 round trip) and $15 per side ($30 round trip) to show this impact.

Using $160 round trip reduces the size of the average winning trade by $160 to $990 ($1150 - $160), and increases the size of the average losing trade to $800 ($640 + $160).

$$ME = [1 + (990/800)] \times 0.61 - 1$$
$$= 2.24 \times 0.61 - 1$$
$$= 1.37 - 1$$
$$= 0.37$$

While we still have a positive expectancy (edge) and will still be profitable, the numbers have been significantly reduced.

Using brokerage of $30 round trip reduces the size of the average winning trade to $1120 ($1150 - $30) and increases the size of the average losing trade to $670 ($640 + $30).

$$ME = [1 + (1120/670)] \times 0.61 - 1$$
$$= 2.67 \times 0.61 - 1$$
$$= 1.63 - 1$$
$$= 0.63$$

Sample size

The other important issue when calculating your edge is sample size. Looking at a small sample size of trades can often produce false results and either lead to high expectations for a system that then collapses, or alternatively poor expectation for a system that actually performs well over the long term. This is caused as a result of runs or strings of losers or winners. If you select a small sample size or data set, the results produced may reflect the fact that the system has simply had a run of losers or winners. This will have an impact either negatively or positively on the results arrived at, but may actually bear no resemblance to the results of the system over the long run.

The past ain't the future ... (yet)

And of course, we must remember the tag line provided with all financial products in these days of over-governance and warnings for the unwary and uneducated—that 'past performance is not an indication of future performance'. We must also realise that back-testing systems and crunching all these numbers can really only provide us with proof of what has happened in the past. No-one can guarantee what will happen in the future, but at least past results can provide us with a guide as to what to 'expect'. It is then up to each of us as managers of ourselves, our money and our systems to take responsibility for our trading decisions and our money management.

What's your edge?

Your edge is defined by the unambiguous entry and exit criteria that determine when you buy and sell in the market. This is your trading system, methodology or trading plan that defines clearly and precisely what you will do and when you will do it.

> Having no 'edge' will manifest itself through making trading errors in the market. Below are some examples, but this list is not exhaustive.
>
> ⇨ Not taking trades that the system has generated through fear of the outcome.
>
> ⇨ Chasing trades after they have bolted and long after a system with an edge provides an entry signal.
>
> ⇨ Taking trades that shouldn't be done by reacting to noise, tips, advice or the opinion of others and that haven't been signalled by the system.
>
> ⇨ Exiting trades too early, too late, on a 'gut feel' or, worse still, not exiting at all.
>
> ⇨ Putting too much capital into certain trades at certain times—gambling on a 'sure thing' that more often than not goes pear-shaped.
>
> ⇨ Putting too little capital into winning trades.
>
> ⇨ Putting too much capital into losing trades.

> ⇨ Having too much capital in the markets when exposure should be minimised.

> ⇨ Having too little capital in the markets when exposure should be maximised.

After making such errors, traders or investors would typically blame a third party for their trading errors such as a broker, an investment manager, a newsletter, the market, their software, their job because they were too busy at the time, the internet, their computer, and so on. That is, they will not take responsibility for their investment outcomes. Instead, they will justify the losses or distort the reasons why they had losses. Because it was not their fault and it was therefore out of their control, their view is they need take no further action to improve for the next time this occurs!

Those who take responsibility take action to change their trading approach. To improve your outcomes you need to change the way you go about your trading or investing decisions. If you always do what you've always done, you will always get what you've always got...

Creating certainty in an uncertain environment

The uncertain and supposedly complex nature of 'the markets' creates all sorts of irrational responses from those trading without an edge. Those who have a trading plan or system with unambiguous rules and a mathematical or statistical edge are able to trade with a high level of confidence. They are able to trust in the outcomes of the system and achieve a level of calmness and certainty not evident in those without such an edge. These traders have moved well beyond the point of focusing on the outcome of each trade and instead focus on the process of applying the rules and money management principles of their edge, confident that the system will deliver the expected results over the long term.

The ultimate measure of the edge for any system is shown by its long-term equity curve. This needs to be steadily rising and have been traded through a diverse range of market conditions to indicate its real performance during live market trading. An edge with a positive mathematical expectation needs to outperform the market net of brokerage and slippage in live trading conditions. An edge also needs to be able to outperform the market averages in up and down markets by deploying money management and risk management techniques that maximise exposure during rising markets, minimise exposure during falling markets and reduce portfolio drawdown during extreme market downturns.

The chart in figure 10.1 depicts the actual equity curve (top line) of a system called SPA3 (<www.intelledgence.com.au>) that has been traded mechanically in real time with unambiguous entry and exit criteria from 25 January 2001, compared with the Australian all ordinaries index (bottom line). The system has traded through the 11 September 2001 terrorist attacks on the World Trade Center, the 2002–2003 bear market, the 2003–2007 bull market and the 2007–2009 global financial crisis bear market.

Figure 10.1: SPA3 hedge system equity curve

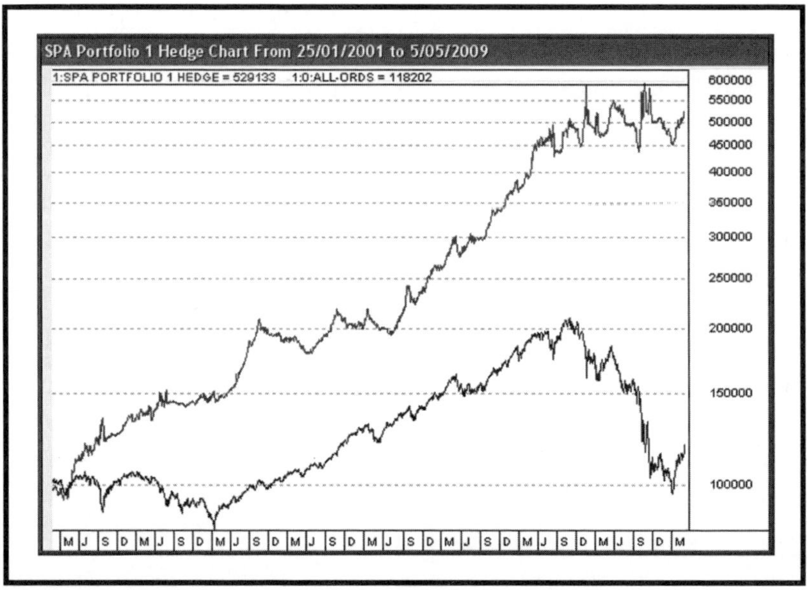

Source: Share Finder

Over this eight-year-and-three-month period, the original starting capital of $100 000 has grown to $529 133 (shown by the top line), while $100 000 invested in the all ordinaries index has grown to $118 202 (shown by the bottom line) and is indicative of managed fund returns over this period.

The $529 133 includes brokerage of $51 131 on 833 closed trades, not including tax (due to Managed Fund and all ordinaries reporting excluding tax). This is a 429 per cent return over eight years or 22.29 per cent compounded per annum compared with the all ordinaries index returning just 18.2 or 2.04 per cent compounded per annum. The positive mathematical expectancy (ME) of the SPA3 system, net of brokerage and slippage, is currently 0.221, over the eight-year period and near the bottom of a 55 per cent retracement in the index, after just over 800 trades — a large sample size.

Keep it real

Crunching the numbers on your trading results will expose them to reality. Do you really have an edge? Are you trading a system that has a positive mathematical expectancy? Are you thinking in terms of winning and losing trades? Or in terms of the overall probability of the successful outcome of the system over time? Once you can clearly identify these numbers and train yourself to accept that the long-term results of a profitable system are way more important than the results of individual trades, you are well on your way to being a disciplined and consistent trader.

Historical performance from research is no guarantee of future performance. When you learn to think in terms of probabilities there is no way that you would trade a system that has negative mathematical expectation based on historical data. Why trade a set of rules that would have either low or no probability of success in the future? You need to have the probabilities in your favour.

Gary Stone is managing director of ShareFinder Investment Services Pty Ltd (<www.sharefinder.com.au>). He has researched and designed proven mechanical investment methodologies. In this chapter, Gary explained the importance of understanding your numbers for successful share trading and investing.

Gary has two active mechanical investment methodologies that are commercially available:

- SPA3 (Sustained Profit Advantage™ 3), a methodology for medium-term active investment in equities, is based on technical analysis techniques. SPA3 has been widely used among active investors in Australia since 1998 and has been released into overseas markets. SPA3 has been extended to a product called SPA3CFD that further enables SPA3 through trading combined equities and CFD portfolios.

- Intelledgence™, a methodology for long-term active investment in equities, is based on technical and fundamental analysis techniques.

Gary is a regular monthly panelist on Sky Business TV's 'Your Money Your Call' program in Australia. He presents at trading and investing seminars, regularly appears on radio, and has a weekly market blog at <www.blog.sharefinder.com.au>. For further information on ShareFinder's products and services, visit <www.intelledgence.com>.

Bet big to lose big

Mistake 11: misusing leverage and margin

*Give me a lever long enough and a fulcrum on
which to place it, and I shall move the world.*

Archimedes

Perhaps one of the most abused and least understood trading tools
are the twin concepts of leverage and trading on margin, often
referred to as gearing. When used effectively and with a complete
understanding of the outcomes that can occur as a result of their
use, both negative and positive, leverage and margin are wonderful
ways to increase returns and enhance the performance of a well-
researched and robust trading system. When not fully understood
and used within the realms of reality the results can be disastrous.
The differentiation between the two is important, as the concepts are
very different, and need to be fully understood. Without a realistic
understanding of these concepts and their implementation, the
outcomes can be horrendous.

Margin or leverage — what's the big deal?

Australian trader, educator and author Christopher Tate explains the difference between leverage and margin:

> I regard leverage and margin as two different concepts. Leverage is the use of a financial instrument such as a futures or options contract to control a larger amount of product than might have otherwise been possible if you were directly trading the underlying instrument.
>
> For example, if I buy a BHP $28 option contract for $1, I effectively have control over 1000 BHP shares for an outlay of $1000 plus costs. If I were to go into the market to buy 1000 BHP at $28 it would cost me $28000 plus costs. The purchase of the option contract has given me the same exposure but for only $1000. This is the basis of leverage—a small outlay enables you to control a large amount of a given instrument. Leverage is also sometimes erroneously referred to as 'gearing'.
>
> Trading on margin or using a margin loan is slightly different but achieves the same outcome. It enables traders to control a larger amount of product than they might otherwise have been able to.
>
> The familiar example of margin trading is the notion of buying a house. All house purchases—except those rare exceptions where someone purchases a house outright for cash—are margin transactions. The homeowner puts up a margin (the deposit) and the rest is borrowed. For example, if I were buying a house for $500000, I would put up a deposit of 20 per cent or $100000 and would borrow the rest. With my $100000 deposit I control a financial asset worth $500000.
>
> So margin refers to the use of borrowed funds to effectively increase your buying power. If we were to put this in the context of a stock trader using a margin loan account then they might purchase a basket of shares using borrowed funds. For example, if I wanted to establish a portfolio with $30000, I might seek to borrow an additional amount of money to increase my purchasing power and the amount of product (shares) I

controlled. If I limited my selection of shares to stocks that had a loan-to-valuation ratio (LVR) of 70 per cent, I would be able to gross my total portfolio up to $100 000. My $30 000 initial margin or deposit is now controlling $100 000 worth of shares.

It is this ability to increase your potential returns that makes both leverage and margin so attractive to traders of all sizes. The use of margin is universal in the trading world. Everyone from mum-and-dad investors to giant hedge funds will use borrowed funds to increase the size of their potential gains. In fact, much of the turmoil in the current market has come about because of forced liquidations of margined positions.

One of the most extreme examples of what can happen to a share price when forced liquidations occur is ABC Learning Centres, whose executives and directors all had margined exposure to their own stock price. As the stock price fell, those with margined positions either had to meet their margin calls or face the forced liquidation of their shares. As shares were forcibly liquidated the price fell, generating more margin calls and further forced liquidations. An awful feedback cycle of falling share prices and forced liquidations triggered even further falls, which triggered further liquidations. The cycle continued until the stock price imploded. Such a disaster is a strong call for the full disclosure by companies of any margin facilities that their directors or staff may have.

Ramp it up ...

The major benefit of using leverage and/or trading on margin is the increased purchasing power of the trader's available capital. As shown in the example above, relatively small amounts of capital can be used to have access to much larger position sizes than would be available to traders if they were to use only the capital or funds they had available. In the futures markets, the same leverage rules apply where significant amounts of a commodity or equity index can be traded by lodging a margin amount with the broker and then trading much larger dollar amounts of the contract. For example, the margin requirement for a futures contract for wheat at the time of writing was US$3375 on a contract with a face value of around US$31 500. This means that the trader is able to trade a US$31 500 face value wheat contract by lodging just US$3375 as margin with the Chicago Board of Trade via their personal futures broker. The result is the possibility to greatly increase returns. At $50 per point, if the price increases by 10 points and the trader is long, a profit of $500 has been made. Having lodged US$3375 to participate in the trade, this represents a return of just under 15 per cent. If the trader had to use the full US$31 500 of the contract's face value to participate in the trade, this would result in a return of a little over 1.5 per cent on the total capital outlaid for the trade. If we assume our trader has a US$50 000 account and has traded conservatively with just one contract, a return on equity of 1 per cent has been achieved from this trade ($500 profit in a $50 000 account). This example shows what happens in the event that the trade has a favourable outcome.

... and smack me down

Of course, the reverse is true if the trade is a loser. In the example above, if the trader suffers a loss of 10 points or $500, this gives a negative return of just under 15 per cent on the amount of margin required for the trade, and around 1 per cent of the trader's overall trading capital. The problem arises when traders are over-leveraged in their account and have not given adequate consideration to what can happen in the event of a major move against their open trade position.

Let's assume that our trader has used the leverage ability of futures trading aggressively, ill-informed and with total lack of understanding of what can go wrong. Like many, this trader uses the available leverage inappropriately and trades too many contracts, through a false sense of self-belief that he is the next great wheat futures trader, or simply by the fact that he is ill-informed or unaware as to what can go wrong. Our trader steps up to the plate and decides to buy 10 contracts, thus using US$33 750 ($3375 margin per contract × 10 contracts) of his available capital to lodge as margin for the trade. Having entered the trade the trader then finds that a few days later the position has moved against him to the point where he has been stopped out of the trade. Unfortunately, the market has 'gapped' through the trader's stop-loss price. Instead of being stopped out with a 10 point loss per contract ($500), the trader realises a loss of 20 points per contract ($1000) as a result of the gap move against the position. The total loss is now US$10 000 ($1000 per contract × 10 contracts). Our trader has suffered a 20 per cent loss in total trading capital, and is left feeling beaten up, and hopefully somewhat wiser from the experience.

A double-edged sword

While this example is a significant loss, it probably wouldn't be considered debilitating. However, there are countless examples of traders using much higher levels of margin or leverage that have resulted in them completely wiping out their trading accounts. For many share and derivatives traders, leverage is a double-edged sword. On one hand it allows us to generate large percentage returns on our available capital. It can also magnify losses and add a larger element of risk for traders who don't fully understand or comprehend the ramifications of trading using margin. Many inexperienced, undercapitalised and underprepared CFD traders have no doubt felt the wrath of the markets when they have been overexposed to adverse market movements. Trading using the margins available from the CFD providers has enabled many people to begin trading using very small amounts of start-up capital. They have then leveraged up these accounts while not fully understanding the consequences of their actions, and have suffered accordingly when the market has moved against them.

Many of these traders had little or no understanding of the consequences of their actions until they experienced the violent correction that occurred in worldwide equity markets during 2008. The following example shows the effect of overusing leverage.

Example 1

Trader Joe opens a CFD trading account with $10000. He begins trading CFDs on the top 20 listed Australian shares with a leverage of 10:1 or 10 per cent. This allows him to take positions with 10 times the face value of the position while only having to lodge a 10 per cent margin. Joe incorrectly believes that his account gives him the ability to have open positions worth $100000. He then goes about buying CFDs based on this premise. Unfortunately for Joe, just as he gets 'his' $100000 spent, the market crashes and his CFD positions are all down by over 15 per cent or $15000. Joe's trading account is wiped out. He has lost his initial $10000, plus he still owes the CFD provider an extra $5000. He is forced to sell out of his open positions and still has to find the extra cash to pay the CFD provider. Joe also signed up and paid his initial $10000 using his credit card, so he now also has a debt on his card to service. And the CFD provider is able to take the extra $5000 from Joe's credit card as well. Joe's dreams are shattered. He has lost his initial capital plus a bit extra that he can't afford to lose — and he has a debt. He thinks trading is for idiots and he hasn't told his wife yet!

Share trading on margin (margin loans)

Just as margin can increase the potential size of a trader's returns it can also increase the size of one's losses. This is a point that is often overlooked in the glossy marketing material that potential investors receive.

Let's return to our share investor with a $100000 portfolio which only has $30000 equity in it. This portfolio has $70000 worth of debt or margin attached to it. The provider of the loan facility will always want its money returned irrespective of market conditions. To make certain that this always occurs, the lender will impose what is known as an LVR. The LVR not only stipulates how much can be borrowed, but also sets the trigger point for any margin call.

Our example tells what effect a fall in the value of our portfolio will be and how much up of a top-up or margin call will be required to stabilise the portfolio at the prescribed LVR.

Let's assume that the value of our portfolio falls to $90 000 from a starting value of $100 000.

Top-up = (margin loan/LVR) – current asset value

= ($70 000/0.70) – $90 000

= $100 000 – $90 000

= $10 000

To bring our level of borrowing back into line with what is required, we would have to add $10 000 to the account.

It might seem unlikely that our portfolio would draw down 10 per cent on a regular basis, but let's assume that our portfolio has a high correlation with the S&P ASX200 Index. By making this assumption we can get an idea of how often we might be faced with such a drawdown.

The chart in figure 11.1 (overleaf) looks at the number of drawdowns that have occurred on the S&P ASX200 Index since January 2000. As you can see, the market has dropped by 10 per cent or more about once per year. It should also be noted that this period includes one of the largest bull markets in history. So you need to be prepared for the possibility that the market will fall and you will suffer a margin call. Such a chart acts as a dose of realism against the overly optimistic projections given by brokers and financial planners when they promote products such as margin loans.

It could be argued that the investor might not have a portfolio that is highly correlated with the underlying index. This is a fairly weak argument because the universe from which shares can be purchased using a margin loan is quite small and is largely drawn from the major indices. Hence, they have a reasonable correlation with the underlying index.

However, it is an interesting exercise to look at the potential drawdown for two of the most popular Australian shares that are included in margin loans: BHP Billiton (BHP), shown in figure 11.2 (overleaf), and Telstra (TLS), shown in figure 11.3 (page 119).

Figure 11.1: chart of ASX200 drawdown analysis

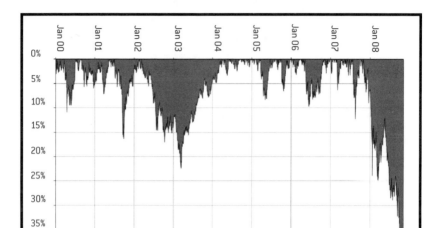

Figure 11.2: BHP drawdown analysis

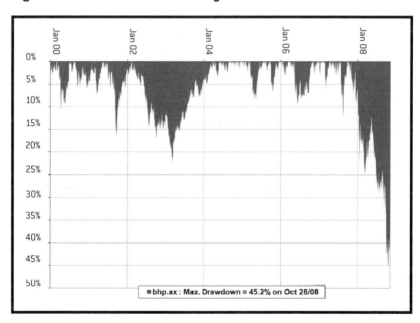

Figure 11.3: TLS drawdown analysis

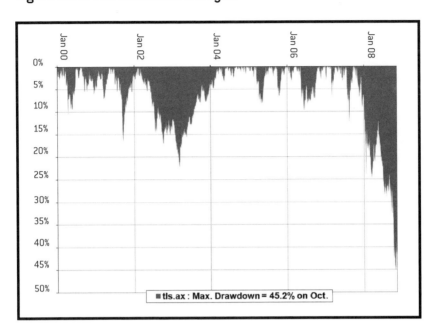

Each of these charts show that stocks can and do fall. It is common among brokers to believe that the law of gravity has been repealed and they express great surprise when things go down. Whenever this does occur, investors generally get the old chestnut of 'good shares always get better'. Unfortunately the market and the person providing the margin loan beg to differ. Consider the chart in figure 11.4 (overleaf) which represents the value of $1 invested into BHP in 1990.

Now we need to view figure 11.4 somewhat cynically. Investors' attention is immediately drawn to the right-hand side of the chart when the value of BHP moved up strongly during the bull market. However, that is not what potential investors should be looking at. They should be looking at the number of times BHP was stagnant for several years and, as per our drawdown analysis, the number of times the stock dropped to such a point that it would trigger a margin call. Investors are often overly optimistic as to their ability to ride out such periods, particularly when they are being reminded of their decreasing equity each day.

Figure 11.4: growth of a $1 investment in BHP since 1990

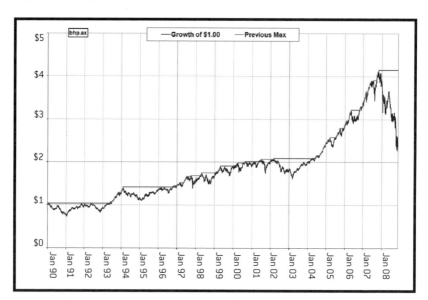

For the reasons outlined earlier, many opt not to borrow the full amount of their portfolio but rather keep their borrowings to a more manageable figure. This is done either by borrowing less, using more equity to establish the facility, or a combination of both. For example, if we change the balance to, say, 50 per cent equity and 50 per cent borrowings, the portfolio would have much greater room to move before we were hit with a margin call.

It also needs to be noted that since this is a loan it will need to be paid back and you need to be certain you can pay it back. You need to take into account the following considerations.

▷ *The security ratio assigned to an asset may change over time.* This means that you may have to suddenly top up your account with extra funds to compensate. However, by being conservative, you can build in a buffer against this.

▷ *Interest rates may rise substantially during the time of the loan.* This issue can be dealt with either by making certain you have surplus cash flow to deal with the additional costs you are incurring, or by fixing the interest rate at a given level. You should ensure that you have enough surplus cash flow to absorb interest payments. You could consider fixing the interest rate on some (or all) of your margin loan to offer protection.

➪ *The income from your investments may fall, leaving you with a cash flow shortage.* You should think about ensuring that you have enough surplus cash flow to cover any income shortfall.

Predicting the market top

It is a wonderfully interesting phenomenon that share trading on margin through the use of margin loans reaches its zenith as bull markets near their peaks. Many would-be traders and investors are lured into them on the promise of participating in the supposedly never-ending growth of equity prices by using only a small amount of their own capital, and borrowing the balance at 'attractive' interest rates. However, it all ends in tears when the market tanks and the trader/investor is left to watch as share prices slide, decimating portfolios and, more often than not, resulting in a margin call.

A margin call is a demand for additional funds by the company providing you with the loan facility. Margin calls traditionally result from a fall in the value of the investor's portfolio, although occasionally they may result from a change in the level of borrowing permitted against a given stock.

It is important to note that this is a demand for additional funds — it is not a request to be taken lightly. Investors generally have 24 hours to respond to the call for additional equity. If the call is not met then the loan provider can and will begin selling down the portfolio to reduce the value of the exposure and to bring the portfolio back into line with their lending guidelines. A forced sell-down should be avoided if possible because the lender will simply issue the instruction to begin selling your holdings at market. If any of these orders hit a thinly traded market, then the prices you achieve during the sell-down may be much worse than if you had undertaken the sell-down yourself in a controlled manner.

Allowing a third party to take control of your investments also demonstrates an unwillingness to deal with the issues at hand. Unfortunately, denial is not an investment strategy and investors should always look to be in control of their financial future. This matter should never be left to a third party since they will have only their interests at heart, not yours.

The simplest way to avoid persistent margin calls is to borrow conservatively. Just because you may be able to gear to a certain level does not mean that you need to gear yourself to this level. Borrowing limits are not compulsory — you may gear your portfolio in the manner that best suits you.

There are only two ways to deal with a margin call once it has been received:

1. Pay up the amount required.

2. Sell down part of the portfolio.

Investors have extremely limited options once the call has been received. It is far better to have some form of defensive plan in place that avoids the calls being received.

Using leverage or margin in trading requires a thorough understanding of both the positive and negative consequences that gearing can create. Ignoring it is not an option, nor is believing that the negative outcomes will not happen to you. They will! It is vitally important to thoroughly understand the implications of using any level of gearing in your trading business. Properly understood and used, gearing can and will substantially increase the returns available to traders and investors. Gearing up a robust and profitable trading system or strategy has the potential to make great results become outstanding. Gearing up a poorly performing system or trading strategy will only serve to wipe it (and you) out quicker than if it were not geared.

Use it wisely and it will be your friend; use it unwisely and it will be your worst enemy.

Christopher Tate is a trading veteran of 30 years. He has had an extraordinary impact on thousands of traders. Bestselling author of *The Art of Trading* and *The Art of Options Trading in Australia*, his brutally honest approach and meticulous pursuit of excellence qualify him as Australia's foremost derivatives trading expert. In this chapter, Christopher explained leverage and margin and the dangers of misusing them.

Christopher has seen all types of markets, traded every instrument available, and profited in every one of them. He is in constant demand for his world-renowned mentor program and keynote speaking skills. Christopher has the skills to help you to radically jumpstart your returns. Unlike most other trainers who teach only theory, Christopher is one of the few people who truly understand what does and does not work in the share market. Register at <www.tradinggame.com.au> for a pack of free trading goodies to help you trade profitably and safely.

What's the time, Mr Wolf?

Mistake 12: confusing time frames and trading strategies

Time is a dressmaker specializing in alterations.

Faith Baldwin

Are you a short-term, medium-term or long-term trader? Are you a mixture of all of these? Or do you have no idea what these terms mean? Despite their constant use in the trading world, what do these terms really mean and why is it important anyway? Veteran US trader and educator Jake Bernstein offers the following definitions:

> There is no hard-and-fast definition. To the day trader, long-term may be a few days. To an investor, short-term may be a few weeks. I use working definitions that are flexible. For me, a short-term trade is about one to 10 days. Medium-term is 11 days to a few weeks and anything longer than a few weeks is long-term. These working definitions apply only to futures. In stocks it's very different. There may be tax implications associated with holding stocks for a minimum length of time. We may need to work around these in order to take advantage of these tax implications.

What's your time frame?

The most important issue is to identify which type of trader you are and the time frame that will suit you and be your best 'fit' with the market. Identifying this is covered in chapter 5. It is also possible to be able to trade multiple time frames across multiple markets once the appropriate skills and levels of confidence to do this have been developed. In this way it is possible to hold some trades open for longer periods, while at the same time having shorter time frame trades occurring—these may even contradict each other in terms of the direction of the trade. To do this requires skills to study the market and identify your trading opportunities across varying time frames. In this way it is possible to be short based on medium- or long-term conditions and set-ups while at the same time being long based on short-term conditions and set-ups.

> Looking at a different time frame is like looking at a piece of art. If you stand very close you will see things that you won't see if you stand further away. If you stand close you may see dots and spots of paint. If you stand far enough away you will see a bigger picture. Either one is okay to do as a trader, but the time frame you select needs to match the time frame that you trade. Too often traders examine all time frames to reach a decision. I maintain that this is not the right way to do things. Markets tell you different things depending on the time frame. A market can be very bullish short term and it can rally strongly within the context of a huge bear market. There is a famous poem entitled *The Blind Men and the Elephant*. I recommend it to all traders. Read it and benefit from its lesson. Trade within a given time frame and make your decisions within the time frame that you are trading. For the most part, analysing multiple time frames in the same market in order to reach a trading decision will lead to confusion. And confusion leads to losses.

'The Blind Men and the Elephant' by John G Saxe

It was six men of Indostan,
To learning much inclined,
Who went to see the elephant,
(Though all of them were blind),
That each by observation
Might satisfy his mind.

The first approached the elephant,
And, happening to fall
Against his broad and sturdy side,
At once began to bawl
'God bless me! but the elephant
Is very like a wall!'

The second, feeling of the tusk,
Cried: 'Ho! what have we here.
So very round, and smooth, and sharp?
To me 'tis very clear,
This wonder of an elephant
Is very like a spear!'

The third approached the animal,
And, happening to take
The squirming trunk within his hands,
Thus boldly up he spake:
'I see,' quoth he, 'the elephant
Is very like a snake!'

The fourth reached out his eager hand,
And felt about the knee:
'What most this wondrous beast is like
Is very plain,' quoth he;
''Tis clear enough the elephant
Is very like a tree!'

The fifth, who chanced to touch the ear,
Said: 'E'en the blindest man
Can tell what this resembles most:

Deny the fact who can,
This marvel of an elephant
Is very like a fan!'

The sixth no sooner had begun
About the beast to grope,
Than, seizing on the swinging tail
That fell within his scope,
'I see,' quoth he, 'the elephant
Is very like a rope!'

And so these men of Indostan
Disputed loud and long,
Each in his own opinion
Exceeding stiff and strong,
Though each was partly in the right
And all were in the wrong!

Moral: So oft in theologic wars,
The disputants, I ween,
Rail on in utter ignorance
Of what each other mean,
And prate about an Elephant
Not one of them has seen.

In order to trade multiple strategies across multiple time frames it is vital that you stick strictly to the rules of each trading system, and not mix up the entry or the exit rules. A trade entered based on the rules for a medium-term hold period must be exited according to the rules of that system, and not confused with the rules for a short-term trade entered in the same market. Often traders will enter, say, a medium-term trade based on the rules of their trading system or strategy. They will then receive an entry signal for a short-term trade in the same market. This may be in the same or opposite direction to the original medium-term trade. The short-term trade does well and they exit with a profit. They then become confused with the medium-term trade and, because it is suffering a short-term move against them, they will then exit that position at a loss, only to then watch as the trade does as they had anticipated but without them involved in the trade and the subsequent profit.

Long and short beans

The example shown in figures 12.1 and 12.2 explains graphically this ability to be long and short in the same market based on different time frames and trade criteria. In this example my medium-term system has triggered a buy signal in beans and I go long. A few weeks later, my short-term system triggers a short-term sell signal in the same market. I am now both long for a medium-term trade and short for a short-term trade in soybeans. The most important issue for me now is to let both trades run their course according to the rules of each system, and not confuse the two. Six days after entering the short trade, I am able to exit this trade with a profit. My long side trade is still open and continues to move in my favour, despite the short-term pull back in price.

Figure 12.1: long beans with a medium-term entry condition ...

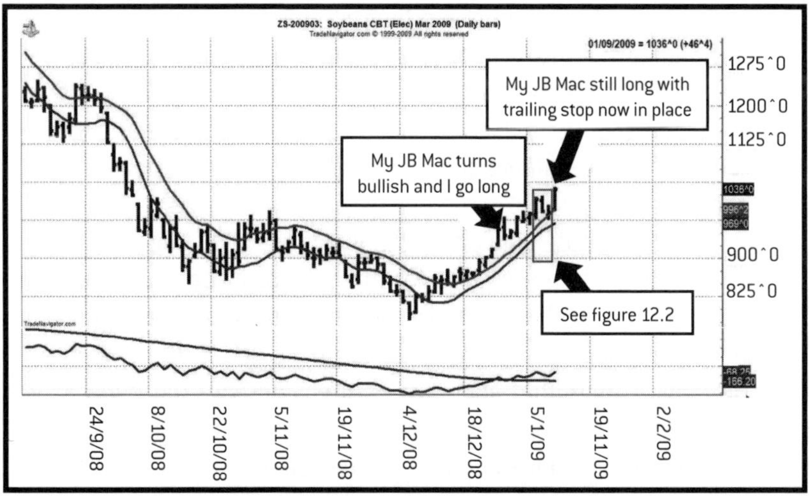

Source: Trade Navigator © Genesis Financial Technologies, Inc.

Figure 12.2: ... and short beans short-term in a medium-term uptrend (long trade still open)

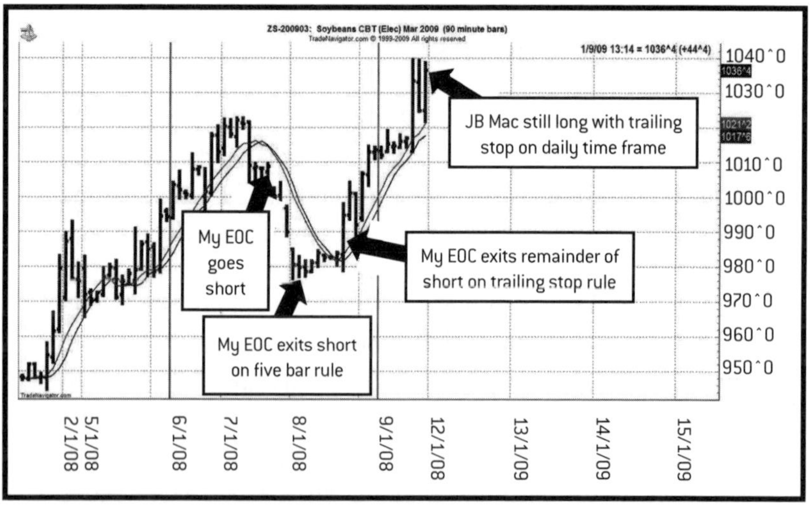

Source: Trade Navigator © Genesis Financial Technologies, Inc.

It is entirely possible to be long in a market for a major move in one contract month and short in a different contract month in the same market for a short-term contra-trend move. There are some traders who believe that all time frames in a market must agree in terms of direction. I vehemently disagree. I can be very bullish on gold or any other market for the long-term and own it as an investment, and still go short for a brief seasonal move down. Keep things simple. Complexity confuses; simplicity succeeds.

There are those who claim that indicators in all time frames must be in the same direction for a trade to be made. They check the daily and weekly charts for synchronicity before they trade. If trading short term, they check the daily and the hourly. To be frank, I think that approach is utter nonsense (no offence intended). It is entirely possible for two or more trades to be in opposite directions in different time frames and for both to make or lose money.

Don't burn the cake

Identifying the time frame you are trading with each trade is vital, as is identifying your trading style and technique and recognising either the time frame that best gels with your personality, available time and available capital, or your ability to trade multiple time frames across multiple markets. There is little point setting out to become a short-term trader if you have a career path that prevents you from watching the price screen intraday and trading these short-term market gyrations. I was once asked by a long-haul transport driver who was often on the road for days at a time if I thought it would be possible for him to be a short-term trader! If you are the type of person who reacts to each and every price move when you have a position open, then you may be more suited to short-term trading, as opposed to a longer term trader who is more interested in end-of-day prices and trends rather than the intraday noise of the market.

> The temptation to mix and match signals is perennial. The human mind strives to create order from chaos—to organise and connect the disparate parts of reality. That effort serves us well in situations that are amenable to an orderly view, since they are not random by nature. There is a reasonable amount of logic in our daily dealings with people and in relationships. In a stable relationship with another person we know that they are having a 'bad day' or a 'small setback' and so we ignore these small blips in the big interpersonal uptrend. However, many traders are unable to translate this understanding to the markets. They panic when there are blips. Those of us who realise that the blips can be traded contrary to the existing trend can profit by them, and we realise that deviations from an existing trend are not necessarily indicative of a change in the trend but rather an opportunity within the trend. To put this on a personal level, if a loved one is having a bad moment (deviation from the trend), we often 'profit' from his or her misery by extending love or assistance. Somehow, traders can't translate that type of behaviour into trading behaviour.

Money and time

The availability of trading capital may also determine one's ability to trade across varying time frames. Those with smaller accounts may simply not have enough capital to have a number of open positions at any one time, and may need to increase their trading capital before they can employ a variety of strategies and trading systems using different time frames.

> Assuming that you have several valid systems and the capital to trade them all, then you can trade them all but in different accounts. I have no issues with that, provided the systems trade based on unique or different underlying concepts or methods. The fact that you may be long in one market in one account and short in the same market in another account is not a conflict as I see it, provided that the systems have different exit and entry signals. At first blush this may not seem logical, but if you think about it, the logic is clear. Assuming you do not have sufficient capital you need to focus and restrict your trades to whichever signal comes first, no matter what the system. Finally, another approach is to determine which systems work best in which markets and to trade that way without duplication.

Clarity is king

It is always best to begin with one strategy initially and then move into trading varying time frames once you have developed the skills and confidence necessary to be able to operate two or more trading strategies simultaneously. The mindset required is one of mental strength, knowledge and conviction. You must be 100 per cent clear on the rules of each strategy and act only according to these rules, without confusing the rules for each system or strategy.

Using a mechanical approach to your trading (see chapter 17) to greatly reduce the emotional involvement with each trade is extremely important for anyone considering trading more than one system or strategy. In this way, trades are simply entered and exited according to the system rules, without any emotional consideration. Many short-term trading strategies can also be automated using the technology available via the internet and electronic trading platforms. The entry, exit and position sizing rules can be code written into the platform and the orders are sent into the market when the conditions to trade are triggered. This automated trading process is ideal for intraday trading systems that may generate and execute a large number of orders during a trading session. Once back-tested and proven to work, the coded system can then fully automate the trading process, removing the need for human involvement, other than to monitor the system and its performance. This has enormous benefits in terms of reducing the emotive nature of this type of trading, as well as freeing up the trader's time to develop and trade other systems and strategies (and have a life).

> It is indeed possible to trade different systems and methodologies across different time frames, but the fact is that most traders have neither the organisational skills nor the trading skills to do this. There is much to be said in favour of three levels of diversification. They are as follows:
>
> 1. diversification across markets
>
> 2. diversification across time frames
>
> 3. diversification across systems.
>
> Ideally this is the best overall approach, but it takes organisation and discipline.

Jake Bernstein is president of MBH Commodity Advisors Inc. and Bernstein Investments Inc. He has authored more than 40 books on trading, investing, investor psychology and economic forecasts. Jake is an active trader in stock, currencies and futures. In this chapter, Jake shared his experience and tips on taking an objective approach to trading time frames.

Jake has developed highly effective trading systems as well as several innovative timing and trend indicators. His technical trading methods are purely objective and specific. His set-up/trigger/follow through (STF) trading model has been adopted by many traders throughout the world. Jake's websites include <www.trade-futures.com>, <www.2chimps. com>, <www.seasonaltrader.com> and <www.patterns4profit.com>.

Where the ^!*# is the exit?

Mistake 13: not having a clearly defined exit strategy

*If you must play, decide upon three things at the start:
the rules of the game, the stakes and the quitting time.*

Chinese proverb

Traders and investors alike are constantly told by all manner of market educators, system providers, authors and every Tom, Dick and Harriet with an opinion on the markets to 'always trade with stops' or to 'know your exit strategy before you place every trade'. The basic premise is that all traders *must* know how and when they will exit each and every trade they undertake.

Despite this constant urging, pleading and even begging, being consistent in the exit decision, be it a stop-loss, profit target, or trailing stop, seems to confound the majority of traders, and cause huge amounts of grief and discomfort. For the majority of traders, taking action to exit trades is perhaps the most difficult part of trading. It is where the majority of screw-ups and agonising occurs. What is it about exits that causes so much anguish and confusion? Why do traders constantly need to be reminded about the importance of exiting trades at a predetermined level?

Trying to out-think the market

Renowned American trader and respected market educator Larry Williams has been trading a wide range of markets for well over 40 years. He has had experience across markets as diverse as butter and eggs when they were traded on the floor of the Chicago Mercantile Exchange (CME), to trading on present-day electronic platforms. Larry offers his view on always having a stop-loss in place at the outset of every trade, which comes from experiencing some substantial losses early in his trading career.

> The reason I trade with an initial stop-loss is to avoid the problem of thinking a market will come back once the trade has gone against me. Trading without an initial stop-loss in place is the most certain way of losing money that I know of. To have a mental or desk stop, kidding or saying to yourself, 'if prices go below that level I will get out of the trade' just doesn't work! The reason for that is once the price does go below that level, if you're long for example, then you still have to fight to get out of the trade because you will look for the price to rally before you attempt to get out of the trade.
>
> The market then maybe stages a bit of a rally and you think, 'great, the trade is now going as I thought it would', so you hang on, still without a stop-loss in place.
>
> The market then tanks again and the trade moves further and further into loss and you continue waiting for a rally to get out of the position. The desperately needed rally doesn't happen and the loss grows and grows and grows. Suddenly, you wake up realising the losses are way beyond what your expectation was. You have now lost a much larger percentage of your bankroll than you ever anticipated. So what do you do? Inevitably, the trade gets cut right at the bottom, the loss is way greater than you originally intended, and you are left mentally and financially bruised and battered. At least that has been my experience ... that has been how I have seen most traders react to a price going below their mental or desk stop.

Getting trampled by cattle

The most distinct memory I have of not getting out at a pre-determined stop is a live cattle trade I had in 1973 (shown in figure 13.1, overleaf). Cattle had been in an uptrend for a long time and my analysis suggested prices were set to go much higher.

I bought quite a few live cattle contracts and the price immediately went towards my stop. I didn't pay attention to that at all because I was very bullish on cattle and my mentor was also very bullish on cattle at the time, so I thought any suggestion that prices could fall was all bull! Instead of getting stopped out and accepting a small loss, I actually bought more contracts. The price then went lower than the stop-loss I had set mental stop' for the second position. To further compound when I bought more contracts. I kept doing this all the way down until eventually I didn't have any more money and the margin calls could not be answered. The market did eventually bounce quite a bit, but of course I had been forced out of the trade by that stage from the need to close out the position and fund the margin calls.

Figure 13.1: live cattle trade with no stop-loss

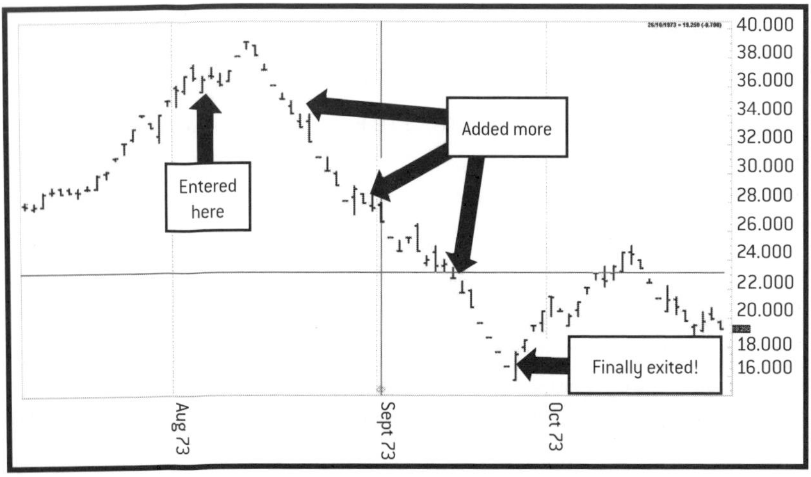

Source: Trade Navigator © Genesis Financial Technologies, Inc.

Mental stops for mental cases

From that trade, in which I lost over $1 million, I learned it is better to get stopped out at the original stop-loss price, and to admit you are wrong early in the piece! I was also fortunate enough to have had quite a good winning streak prior to this large losing trade, so I was not wiped out. From that point on, I have always traded with a stop-loss in place. As a result, by the end of the year I had made back more than the amount I lost in the cattle trade. This is not just a mental or desk stop, but either a verbal order given to my broker, or a stop-loss resting in the market if I am trading the particular market on an electronic platform. Incidentally, the reason they are called mental stops is because you are considered a 'mental case' if you use them, and do not employ the services of a broker to work your stops for you, or place them yourself via an electronic platform.

I just wanna get it right!

As humans we want to be 'right'. We are hard-wired from an early age to be correct and get the answers right. At school we are constantly 'taught' that being right is good and being wrong means you are stupid. As a consequence, we don't want to be proven wrong and we have a tendency to hang on, often in vain, to this belief system. As traders this can be damaging both mentally and financially. Traders want to believe that all their hard work in analysing the market, making an entry decision and then placing the trade will result in the trade making a profit, and proving to themselves and perhaps others that they were right.

However, it is far better to accept early in a trade that you are wrong, exit on your stop, and move on to the next trade. In this way you are reinforcing to your mental faculties that: it is okay to be wrong; it doesn't actually cause that much grief; and, in actual fact, no-one else really knows or cares anyway. Yet if you hang on and try to prove to yourself that you are right, then the results can often be very messy. You can turn a loss of a few hundred bucks (perhaps the value of a few cartons of beer) into something much, much worse (like the next six months' mortgage payments). Heaven forbid you are then forced into telling your spouse that 'Honey, you know that holiday we had planned on the deserted tropical island? Well, we have to change our plans a little ...'

Shooting for a target

Similar to setting stops, when aiming for a profit target to exit a profitable trade (usually the domain of short-term traders) there is always the temptation to override the 'system'. You may want to hang on to a winning trade that has already reached the target price in the belief that it will go higher still, resulting in an enormous profit that will fulfil the dream of a five-star world trip. This may be the case occasionally, but as professional traders know, grabbing the predetermined profits is what short-term trading is all about. Hanging on to trades for longer periods in an attempt to squeeze every last drop of profit out of the trade is not what short-term trades are aiming for. Doing this usually ends in frustration and anger. By contrast, long-term trend followers aim to capture these big moves, and need to employ a trailing stop methodology as discussed below.

The trader and the shoe salesman

Here, Larry Williams shares his experience of ignoring profit targets.

> The opposite to ignoring a stop-loss is equally true when prices are rallying and reach a predetermined profit target price where you should get out at that particular point in time. Hope again sets in. You begin hoping prices will go higher so you don't get out of the trade and, of course, that's when the market starts to decline and you miss making the profits you could have taken.

The analogy I like to use here is that you own a shoe store and someone comes in to buy a pair of shoes from you and says, 'yes I would like those'. You don't suddenly say to him, 'well I want more money for them now'. You are pleased to get your price for them. But when it comes to trading we always want to get a little bit more and the temptation is to hold on for higher prices when we should be taking our profits. Then we have compounded our problem because now we know we should have got out at the higher price and prices are coming down, so what do we do? We wait for the rally that never comes and now we have to scramble out of the position. I would rather take a profit at a target for a predetermined exit price. If prices go higher, so be it, I can't get upset too much about that because I got out of the market with what I wanted—a profit. I sold my 'shoes' for what I thought was a good price. The fact that someone else can get out at a higher price has no bearing on my trade.

Getting greedy for coffee

An example from my own trading (shown in figure 13.2) will help with understanding this. In late June 2008 I was long on coffee which went to my target and I didn't get out of the trade. There was a well-defined exit at 160.05, based on my target shooter concept (included in Trade Navigator software). The price went exactly to that point and I should've taken my profits. But, just like a beginner trader, I got greedy and started thinking that the price for coffee would go much higher, so I did not get out at my target. However, I did use a trailing stop so I was stopped out on my trailing stop about 10 full points lower than my original target. This meant I gave back about $1500 profit for each contract I was long … that's money that rightfully belonged to me that I didn't get because I got greedy.

Figure 13.2: coffee trade with profit target

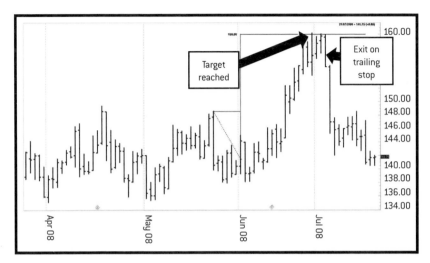

Source: Trade Navigator © Genesis Financial Technologies, Inc.

Using a trailing stop

Even trend followers using trailing stops and aiming for large trades over extended periods of time can be tempted by the mistress of greed. Despite the trailing exit point following the trade, and predefining the exit price once the trend changes, too often they are tempted to override this exit point in the mistaken belief that they know better than the market. Traders want to believe that this is only a minor correction before the trend resumes and their trade will continue on its way to generate the profit they need to retire in the Bahamas. But, inevitably the trade tanks, and they are left holding a 'long-term investment'—hanging on to the position hoping 'one day' it will return to a price at which they can at least recover their cost. Alternatively, they sell out at a point way below their initial exit and a once-profitable trade is now (at best) a break-even trade or (at worst) a loss trade! Larry's live cattle trade in figure 13.1 is a classic example.

The eternal optimist

Larry's examples serve as a reminder of the issues around exit rules. While these two trades are 35 years apart, they are timeless examples of the issues faced by all traders—in particular those trading in a discretionary manner or using arbitrary decision-making processes in their trading. Problems arise as soon as exit rules become discretionary. When greed raises its ever-present head, we are forced to bargain with it in an attempt to justify our actions. We then get into negotiating with ourselves about what we 'should' do and the resulting confusion and mayhem create turmoil in our minds as we struggle to master our thoughts. This always occurs in the heat of the moment when our emotions and adrenalin are operating at extreme levels. This is not a good place from which to be trading, as I'm sure many of you can attest to. The problem of overriding exit rules seems to stem from the fact that, as traders, we are eternally optimistic about our trades and trading prowess. This is evident in Larry's overview of trader personalities and why we are so often tempted to override our predetermined exit strategies:

> There are two types of people in the world it seems: pessimists and optimists. Traders are optimists and always think things will work out for them. That is the only personality that would dare trade!
>
> Of course, the problem is, when in a loss, their positive nature overrides reality. They think things will get better, but they don't always, so losses grow when the market is moving against them as they wait for conditions to improve—that can be a long and costly wait.
>
> When in a profitable trade, these same people exhibit another tendency of all traders: greed. These greedy personality types hang on hoping for more profits. Enough is not enough for them so they hold on to eternal hope instead of doing what a businessperson would do: take profits.
>
> Eventually, traders realise they she must learn to take losses and control greed, or they will get tapped out of this business. This is not an easy endeavour for people who avoid reality.

Why trade with exit rules?

Without doubt, exit rules are frustrating, annoying and challenging at times. These feelings are not limited to beginner traders either. For all the frustrations associated with exit rules, profit targets, and loss-preventing stops in particular, there is one major reason traders must always employ them. This is the simple fact that without a stop-loss and trade exit system you will inevitably lose money and even perhaps be forced to give up trading.

The use of discretionary exits is a trap for the foolhardy and the unwary. While it may occasionally produce a winning trade it will not be consistent and repeatable over a large data set or long trading career.

Stops preserve our capital when we are wrong and keep us in the game to enable us to participate in the winning trades. Despite being frustrating and often annoying, they allow us to keep playing. They are our 'get-out-of-jail-free card'. Without stops, your engagement with the market will be not much short of gambling, and you will eventually lose all your trading capital.

When planning your exit rules, profit targets and loss-preventing stops, keep these points in mind:

▷ *Always* trade with an initial stop-loss in place. This is the only way to preserve your trading capital and to stick around long enough to become a successful and profitable trader.

▷ Making exits as mechanical as practically possible takes away the need to make subjective decisions when under pressure, reduces the emotional attachment to each trade, and leads to a much less stressful trading environment.

▷ Trailing stops result in you giving back some theoretical profit, but will also keep you involved in a trending market for a longer period of time in an attempt to capture larger trend moves over longer periods of time.

▷ Profit targets are used by short-term traders aiming for a predefined profitable exit from a trade. When shooting for a target, *always* exit at your target price and ignore the temptation to chase higher prices.

▷ Use a trading plan. Have your trading rules predefined, written down and *stick to them!* (See chapter 3.)

▷ Document your trades and learn from your mistakes. As you develop as a trader you will be able to readjust and get on with the business of trading much stronger from the experience.

▷ Always trade with appropriate risk management and money management rules (see chapter 8).

The magic ingredient?

Larry Williams knows that being successful in the trading business requires a strict set of rules for engaging the market, of which exit rules are of paramount importance. But a pinch of acceptance and a large dose of reality go a long way too.

> The best way to avoid this trap of not exiting correctly, I think, is to make your exits as mechanical as you possibly can and to realise that the market is full of imperfections. There is simply no way you're going to get every penny out of the market. We don't need to stuff up these winning trades by overlaying them with our personal bias and the ever-present demons of fear and greed. To me, it's all about greed. The reason I didn't get out of the coffee trade, taking a nice profit, is because I got greedy and thought it would go higher. The reason I lost so much money in cattle was I got greedy and thought prices would come back and I didn't want to exit the trade at a loss.
>
> What I have learned and continue to re-learn from my trading experience is simply to follow the rules you have and don't deviate from them. Above all, I think it is learning the acceptance of how erratic and frustrating the markets can be. No-one can call the high and no-one can call the low. We should be pleased to take chunks out of the middle and not be worried about money we can't make to begin with. We need to stick stringently to our initial stop losses and accept them gladly when they take us out of a trade early. Hanging on and hoping

is a sure-fire way to become a big-time loser. They say speed kills … greed is a common death merchant of all traders.

Larry Williams has been trading futures and commodities for well over 46 years. He is the most highly regarded and well-known short-term trader in the world. He has more trading and investing books on the market than any other futures trader. In this chapter, Larry gave his advice on how to properly select your trading exit strategy.

Larry has taught thousands to correctly trade the markets. He has won many trading championships, and has been the only futures trader in the world to repeatedly trade $1 million of his own money at live seminars around the globe. In 1966 Larry developed his famous timing tool, Williams %R. This tool still is published daily in many major financial papers and is a standard indicator provided on trading websites and software programs. In between trading, researching and developing trading tools, teaching and writing, Larry managed to run twice for the US Senate as well as 70 marathons. He holds a higher degree in archaeology and has manned several expeditions. A full list of Larry's books and achievements can be found at <www.ireallytrade.com>.

But the guy on TV said it would go up tomorrow!

Mistake 14: listening to the advice of media and others

I wish to say what I think and feel today, with the proviso that tomorrow perhaps, I shall contradict it all.

Ralph Waldo Emerson

The globalisation of the world through the electronic media and the internet has led to a proliferation of TV shows, chat rooms and websites devoted solely to the delivery of financial information. It seems every time you turn on the TV or pick up a newspaper, someone is offering an opinion about the markets, the economy, the price of gold, the reasons for the current state of the financial system and a multitude of other finance-related topics. In short, the world is awash with financial news and opinion.

These media 'talking heads' are happy to voice their opinions on everything—commodities, stock prices, currency valuations—and these opinions generally change on a whim. Most market commentators tend to be either reactionary or predictive in their opinions. They will comment on a price move well *after* it has occurred or try to predict the future direction of prices with any available data that supports their viewpoint. These latter commentators tend to fall into the 'hero' category—vainly attempting to be the hero that calls the bottom or top of a market move, so they can shout 'I told you so' to anyone who will listen.

A major issue with these market commentators, analysts, brokers, economists, and anyone else expounding a theory on future prices is the lack of accountability. It is quite common to hear these supposedly well-informed opinion givers expressing negative and bearish opinions and commentary one week, only to be positive and bullish the next week, with no reference to their comments of the previous week. This chopping and changing of opinion and lack of accountability needs to be considered by anyone using these opinions as the basis for their decisions to buy and sell.

Having a well-researched and tested system or strategy for engaging the markets is a big step towards success in any trading business. This point has been stressed by every one of the traders interviewed in this book. Despite this, many traders and investors still look to the media for market news and information and often base their trading decisions around these stories and opinions.

It must be right—I saw it on TV

Glen Larson, President of Genesis Financial Technologies (<www.genesisft.com>)—suppliers of the Trade Navigator software program—offers some thoughts as to why people are drawn to these various media and market commentators either to make their trading decisions, or to search out information that supports their opinion and their open positions in the markets.

> If investors are unsure of which actions they should be taking, fear becomes the main driving force in their decisions. If traders do not know what to do, they will look to see what their friends, broker or the advisers on TV are saying. Thus, the easiest way to trade is to follow the crowd. Many people, traders included, do what everyone else is doing—they follow the herd. It feels safe; after all, if everyone is doing it, it can't be wrong. These guys are on TV so they must be experts! Unfortunately, too many traders begin to doubt their own abilities. They begin to

fear that the successful traders have special characteristics that they don't have, which is the wrong belief. They believe those who have succeeded must have sprung up naturally and have some natural or innate talent and that they can't duplicate their success.

A common human trait is to find validation or confirmation in our decisions. Most people aren't lazy; it's just too hard to go against the crowd. After all, we are trained from our initial schooling to conform to the rules, conform to what everyone is supposed to do. It carries over into the rest of our lives. We find it so hard to go against the crowd rules or expectations. As traders this can lead us into the trap of seeking confirmation that we are 'doing the right thing', rather than concentrating on applying the rules of our system or trading methodology.

It's also a bit of 'getting something for nothing' type approach. How can I get rich without spending the time or making the effort? That's the reason so many people buy systems that are sold on TV. They believe they will double their money when they get a green- or red-light signal with no thought or action. They are both unsure of themselves and/or looking for the easy road to success. When it sounds too good to be true, it usually is. Just look at the Madoff fiasco. In 2009, Bernard L Madoff was convicted of running a multibillion-dollar fraud scheme—perhaps the largest in Wall Street's history. Regulators have not yet verified the scale of the fraud, but the criminal complaint filed against Mr Madoff in the federal court in Manhattan reports the estimated losses at $50 billion.

Hey, it's not my fault, I only drank 10 beers!

Stepping up to the plate to implement a trading strategy and continue to apply it with discipline, consistency and patience requires traders to accept responsibility for each and every decision they make, the trades they take, and the outcomes of these trades—win, lose or draw. It requires us to think in terms of probabilities and to understand the 'numbers' associated with our chosen strategy (see chapter 10). Taking responsibility for all the decisions that we make in our lives, not just our trading decisions, is an essential fact of life that is being slowly eroded by the society in which we live, and the ease with which ill-informed decisions and their negative outcomes can be easily assigned to someone else. It is easy to blame someone else when we act irresponsibly or take inappropriate courses of action that have an impact on others' lives.

Traders who lack the discipline and courage to accept responsibility for their own actions will seek to apportion blame for losing trades, losing streaks and poor performance to anyone or anything other than themselves. This breeds reliance on 'support' from the guy on the TV with a daily market commentary, a newsletter or internet chat room. When all is going well it is easy to compliment yourself for being a great trader and having wisely chosen your informant. When it all goes pear-shaped, this same person then easily becomes the enemy and can be blamed for all the bad trades, lack of consistency or any other trading mistake. The responsibility has been abdicated to a third party, thus making it no longer your fault when it all ends in tears.

> There is always an element of fear and excitement with the markets. You can win big and, unfortunately, lose big as well if you are ill-prepared and ill-equipped. This creates a potential adrenaline junkie's dream, just as scaling cliffs or jumping from aeroplanes can. The key to this big win/lose situation is to recognise responsibility for choices. As traders we have everything to gain and everything to lose. If we fail to recognise that fact, we are deceiving ourselves.
>
> The hard reality of trading the markets is that our decisions are quickly validated to be good or bad, right or wrong, winners or losers. That's very hard for some people to handle. We have to accept responsibility for our decisions; it's very black and white. On the whole, people are challenged by accepting responsibility for their actions. Take a look at how many lawsuits there are against bars or nightclubs where a person got drunk and sued the owners for letting them drive drunk.
>
> By allowing others to manage their money, trading decisions or investments, people get to pick someone else to assume

responsibility for all their trading and market-related decisions. They also will generally pick someone who is famous or someone who is being used by a lot of other people. So they get two benefits. First, confirmation that they are 'right' by doing what others have done; and second, the ability to pass along their responsibility for managing their money, while trying to participate in the adrenaline excitement of trading.

The real psychological issue is that, when returns go bad, the trading system goes into a drawdown, or the manager or 'guru' loses all their money, they can blame someone else for not being good enough. In doing this, they have abdicated responsibility for their own stupidity to a third party.

Practising and practising the violin

A central theme of this book is that of developing the skills necessary to become competent and professional in your engagement of the market, and to treat your trading endeavours as a business. Successful traders implement strategies that work and have a proven positive statistical advantage over the long term. They have also worked hard on developing both their trading strategies or systems and the mindset of a trader. For most, this has involved countless hours of research and hard work. They have practised implementing trades and testing their ideas and strategies through hours spent studying charts, interactions and price moves, and back-testing and number-crunching using computers and software programs. Just as in any of life's endeavours, there is no 'easy way'. From professional surfers to the highest level neurosurgeons, all are dedicated to the task at hand and spend not only years learning and then honing their skills, but countless hours continually practising and refining their abilities. Trading is no different.

One of the best examples for traders to consider comes from a recent study conducted by K Anders Ericsson at the elite Berlin Academy of Music.[1]

---

1   KA Ericsson, RTH Krampe & C Tesch-Romer, 'The rule of deliberate practice in the acquisition of expert performance', *Psychological Review* 100, no. 3 (1993); pp. 363–406.

Ericsson divided the school's violinists into three separate groups: the stars (those expected to excel); the good performers; and the group that was not expected to ever play professionally. All violinists were about five years of age when they started playing. All groups practised about the same amount of time — two to three hours a week. Those who began to practise about six hours or more a week began to excel. This same pattern continued up until the age of 20. The elite performers (in all groups) were practising over 30 hours a week, some almost totalled 10 000 hours by age 20. Those who remained good players practised a total of about 8000 hours, and the future music teachers a total of 4000 hours. When compared with professional pianists, they saw the exact same pattern. The professionals steadily increased their practice time every year. The striking thing about Ericsson's study was that he and his colleagues couldn't find any 'naturals' — musicians who floated effortlessly to the top while practising a fraction of the time their peers did. Nor could they find any 'grinds' — people who worked harder than everyone else, yet didn't have what it takes to break into the top ranks. Their research showed that what distinguishes one performer from another is how hard he or she works. That's it. And what's more, the people at the very top don't work a little harder than everyone else, they work much, much harder.

To be successful, traders need to spend time trading and back-testing their ideas. In the initial stages this 'trading' can be paper trading or simulated trading using a program such as Trade Navigator that allows orders to be traded in 'simulation' with the real market. Also, they need to become focused and disciplined in their trading pursuits. Just as the violinists who took the extra responsibility to practise more than their counterparts were the ones to reach professional heights, so it is with traders. Those who put in the hours of practice and hard work, and take responsibility for all their trading and life decisions will reach heights that others will only ever dream of.

The best way to learn and educate yourself is to spend time with charts. Copy the methods of educators who actually make money trading. Not someone who has a slick brochure that promises to make you a millionaire next week, but someone with a proven trading record of consistent profitable results over the long term. Learn from several educators then spend time trading. There is no need to reinvent the wheel or method by yourself.

Also, this trading time doesn't initially need to be in real time or with real money. I believe time in front of charts studying price moves and chart patterns and making decisions about what to do is what makes a trader successful. The more time spent doing this analysis, the more you will learn, not just about price action but also about your own psychology and interaction with the market. That's why we put together two methods of replaying the market for our Trade Navigator users: a trade simulator and a trade replay function. In addition, we provide back-testing modules that let traders test their ideas without risking a cent. You also have to know the maths of your trades. This includes win-to-loss ratios, size of profitable trades, money management skills, and the appropriate use and placement of stops. You gain an insight into all this information through back-testing, replaying the markets, paper trading and real trading.

I always hear the statement that paper trading isn't the same. True, but then why does Tiger Woods spend so much time at the practice range? It isn't the same as a real game. Same with trading. You have to know what you will do in different market conditions. Professionals practise their skills over and over again, perfecting their technique in a range of conditions and situations, so they will be well prepared when they encounter these conditions in a competition. In the words of Michael Jordan, 'Being a pro is practising when you don't want to'.

I can't stress this enough: back-test your ideas, spend time with your charts and spend time trading. That is how you will learn and prosper, not through watching someone on TV providing you with an opinion on what will happen. These are only opinions that will chop and change in line with the prevailing market conditions, crowd thinking or vested interests of their employer.

153

A good tradesman never blames his tools

Having the right tools for the job is an important part of any trading business. This includes a computer and an analysis software program that will enable you to scan the market for trading opportunities and allow you to back-test trading strategies, theories and ideas, crunch the numbers and produce a report showing the outcome of these ideas. This program must also allow you to test your strategy via a simulated trading environment, or the ability to 'replay' past trades to watch how they unfold. Coupled with an independent view of the world, the educated trader has no need to be bothered with the views expressed by the supposed media experts. These 'experts' merely have the job of sensationalising the news to improve ratings and advertising revenues for the network that employs them. It is also essential to stay focused, remain positive and fully understand the nature of the trading environment.

> Trading is the hardest business in the world. Traders are always wrong. They either have too few contracts on a winning trade, or too many on a losing trade. They get in or out too early or too late. Mentally, it becomes so easy to beat ourselves up because of our trades and then to go in search of an easy option—like that guy on TV last week who said wheat was about to rally or BHP shares were about to fall. It's easy to think that someone else knows more than us, but in all honesty they probably don't—they just have a profile that makes it appear that way. When we can recognise that we will never be perfect, expect to have losses, expect to make mistakes trading and still expect positive returns, we will become successful. If not, it's easy to be driven nuts by the markets.

Glen Larson is president of Genesis Financial Technologies Inc. A trained engineer, Glen later applied his engineering and mathematical skills in the financial analysis arena, forming Genesis and developing the Trade Navigator software program. Glen has over 25 years of trading and programming experience.

Glen has participated in seminars across the globe, from Russia to Europe, South America, Australia, Singapore and India. He has developed partnerships with many world-renowned traders and major financial institutions and brokerages. These unique relationships and experiences have allowed Glen to identify trading edges that have been built into the Trade Navigator Platform.

Half price and still too expensive

Mistake 15: averaging down

Forewarned, forearmed; to be prepared is half the victory.

Miguel de Cervantes

As a retail purchaser there is absolutely nothing better than getting a 'bargain'. This applies to buying anything, from a shirt that we picked up at a 'buy-one-get-one-free sale' to negotiating the purchase price of a house down 20 per cent in our favour. We just know we have got a great deal and we are happy to tell anyone who will listen. This desire to pay anything other than full price for any item appeals to a deep-seated feeling of victory over the seller that resides in all of us at some level. Unfortunately, it can work against us in the trading arena. The price of a stock or futures contract that was $20 and is now $10 is not necessarily 'cheap'. Nor is it a good deal if it subsequently drops to $5. The punters that fall for this fallacy are victims of the often touted but ill-advised theory of 'averaging down' or dollar cost averaging. Anyone participating in this activity has little or no understanding of risk management, money management, bear markets and trend recognition.

The story usually goes that if a stock that was trading at, say, $20 is now $15 then it must be good buying. If it falls to $10 then it is cheap, and at $5 it's an absolute screaming bargain. As each parcel of shares has been purchased at a lower price, then the 'average' price is much lower than if the whole lot had been purchased at a higher price. The big problem is that stocks can and do go to zero. The recent bear market in global equities saw a number of once 'market darlings' wiped out — their share prices reduced to zero and removed from the exchange on which they were trading. Anyone holding shares in these companies is now holding a worthless asset, despite having bought it when prices were cheap. Not such a great 'bargain' after all.

Australian trader, author and market commentator Tom Scollon offers his views on this age-old and ill-informed practice of averaging down:

> The concept of averaging down in a falling market is ridiculous. Sure, you may have a lower buy-in price, but what is that worth when the price of the stock goes to zero? It is a theory built on the blind self-belief that markets will always rise and stock prices will always recover. This does not always happen, and this practice can cost a lot of people a lot of money if they blindly throw good money after bad thinking they are buying a bargain. It is not only ill-advised and ill-prepared 'mum and dad' investors that fall for the idea either. Some very high profile, wealthy people have lost lots of money buying into companies they thought were 'cheap', only to see prices get smashed even further. Some even purchase huge quantities of shares in their own listed companies in a vain attempt to prop up the share price, and watch helplessly as the market continues to wipe billions of dollars off the value of the company.
>
> Recently a high-profile Australian businessman admitted to losing in excess of $1 billion buying stock in his listed company. To his credit, the guy spoke openly about his foolhardiness to buy more as his stock price continued to slide.
>
> In global investing language this is called dollar cost averaging, but for some existing dominant shareholders in any company there can be other motivations for buying more of

your own stock. This can be blind belief in oneself, it can be a belief that you can prop up your company's share price alone or with a small group of friends, or it can be sheer desperation to save what is left in your existing shareholding, especially if it is leveraged. I am not saying that these motivations exist in every case, but they are common reasons why investors pour more money into an asset declining in value.

I am also reminded of a fund manager I spoke to recently who was telling me that the price of shares in one of the major merchant banks would hold up because its key management had deep pockets. The price of that stock is down over 30 per cent since that conversation. Basic principle: don't follow a falling share price for any reason—no matter how much cash you have—as the market is going to deal with that stock in a way only markets can. For all you know, that could be in a very severe manner.

The chasm of despair

The big issue with a falling market is that we can never know where and when it will end. Despite the urgings of brokers and other advisers with a vested interest in encouraging people to buy in falling markets, prices can be forced lower and lower by the sheer weight of sellers wanting to get out at any price. There are countless examples of brokers, gurus and other so-called experts attempting to pick the bottom of the market who become remarkably silent when prices tumble further and further into the abyss.

Downtrending markets are like a huge glacial crevasse. You may fall in and land on a ledge several metres below the surface. Hanging on for your life, you suddenly feel your grip loosen and you drop several metres lower before landing on another small ledge. You are frightened but not totally distraught because you can still look up and see the sky. Once again though, your strength wanes, your grip loosens and you tumble further into the abyss. You finally 'discover' the bottom after another bone-jarring fall that pitches you into the inky blackness with only a small sliver of daylight way above you somewhere. Perhaps you are fortunate enough to be rescued, make it to the surface to relive your ordeal and vow never to repeat the activity that caused the accident in the first place. Or maybe you're not.

Bear markets are like this. They will drop a bit, consolidate for a while, and have everyone convinced the worst is over, only to drop again as the ledge gives way and the sellers regain control. This may happen several times with various experts calling for the bottom each time one of these ledges is reached. Unfortunately, we don't know we have reached the bottom until some time later when we can all look back with authority and say when it occurred! Those who average down during these times will be punished by the market, many losing substantial sums of money in the process. Some may make it out alive, but many won't. Those using leverage will be particularly hard hit as they will be forced to sell shares and maybe even other assets and investments to meet the margin calls required to fund their deteriorating, over-leveraged share market positions. It is very difficult to know the extent of any bear market and to contemplate the range of scenarios that may unfold. It may be a short, sharp drop and we are rescued at the first ledge, or it may be an extended descent into a seemingly bottomless pit.

Riding the trend

Trend recognition is vital to success in any trading and investing activity. Reduced to its simplest form, technical analysis can be defined as buying in uptrends and selling in downtrends, or 'if it's going up, buy it; if it's going down, sell it'. Yet this simple and straightforward approach eludes many as they either strive to apply too many technical indicators, employ the often-flawed use of fundamental analysis, or simply have no idea what they are doing, deferring all their financial decisions to a broker or financial adviser, who has as much idea about trading and investing in the markets as the average ant.

Averaging into the price of a share or futures contract position during a bull market when the general trend is up makes sense.

But it is a foolhardy approach in a bear market when prices are getting smashed. Being able to recognise the price trend is extremely important. The majority of stock market participants adopt a buy-and-hold strategy and convince themselves that they are in it for the long term. This is the line that brokers pedal to encourage people to average down during downtrends. They push the line that the stock is cheap, and in the long term will be great buying at these levels. A cursory glance at a few share price charts may convince people that this is not always the case. Many stocks that reach dizzying heights during bull markets are often wiped out during bear markets. It is impossible to know what will happen in the markets. Many companies that appear to be sound are often the ones that are wiped out. This is the big problem with using fundamental analysis — relying on the figures supplied by the companies to the market, which may not always be a true reflection of what is really happening internally and (more importantly) in the future. Fundamental data is mainly historical and thus by definition is not forward-looking. This can be very misleading.

If you want my advice ...

For many reasons, people are happy to listen to the advice of others when it comes to their financial matters. This philosophy tends to work well in bull markets, but not so well in falling markets. Everyone can be a hero when prices are rising, but not many are willing to take responsibility when prices are falling. There are also a lot of potential 'heroes' out there — trying to be the ones who picked the market bottom, or advised their clients to buy a particular stock at $5 and now it's back over $10, but these stories are few and far between. In reality, the vast majority who attempt this get beaten into submission by the power of the market.

People are far too reliant on the advice of brokers and other advisers. These guys continue to push the fundamental analysis line of investing for the long term because they are salespeople. Their incomes are created from commissions on the brokerage they generate or from fees and commissions from the funds and products they sell. The majority of people do not get strategic advice anymore. Long gone are the days when the broker or adviser had an intergenerational relationship with families and the advice and strategies were considered over a long time frame. Not only are markets much more dynamic these days, but these relationships no longer exist. Listening to broker advice is throwing away your independence, freedom and propensity to think and act for yourself—it is a blind philosophy and a flawed strategy.

Take the money ... and wait

Traders using technical analysis are able to use a multitude of indicators and charting tools to develop entry and exit techniques to enter and exit trades according to the rules of their system or trading methodology. Most fundamental investors relying on old, manipulated and, at times, questionable data and information do not have these skills. Relying on this information they are more often than not the ones who are drawn into the averaging down trap. Technical traders and those with a trading plan know when it is time to exit trades either on initial stop losses, trailing stops or profit targets. They are able to exit trades as and when required and know not to re-enter the market until their desired set-up conditions are met. In this way they do not hold onto losing positions, and are never drawn into averaging down. Disciplined traders will sit on cash until market conditions again become suitable for their trading strategy, or employ multiple strategies across multiple markets to profit from moves in other markets.

An emotional train wreck

Failing to get out of trades, averaging down into losing positions and hanging on to positions in a bear market not only erode your physical capital but also your emotional and psychological capital very quickly. It is much better to get out of the market when your stops are hit or according to the rules of your trading plan than to stay locked into losing positions. Averaging down only further compounds the emotional attachment you have to every move the market makes.

Holding on is a dumb move. If you get out you can relax and remain detached from the market. You don't have to worry every day about what the market will do. If you aren't holding on to any positions it really doesn't matter what the market does. You can relax and wait patiently to get back into the market with the capital you have preserved by sitting on the sidelines. By comparison, those who have held on, or have been buying into falling stocks, are nervous, tense, stressed out and watching the market's every move.

Eventually they reach a point where they are completely wrecked. When market conditions change and buying opportunities once again present themselves, these guys are so psychologically and financially drained they aren't able to participate. They have run out of money, and emotionally they are fearful of taking another beating at the hands of the market. Inevitably, they wait and wait for the market to prove to them that it is once again a 'nice' place to be, and once again end up getting involved at the high end of the risk curve. Then the process repeats itself.

The emotional roller-coaster associated with remaining in losing positions is extremely taxing. Feelings of euphoria when the market makes a brief rally are quickly annihilated by an engulfing fear that occurs when more money is lost. It is very hard to make clear and objective decisions when you are consumed by fear. These negative emotions grip you and irrational behaviour reigns supreme.

A far better strategy is to use technical analysis, have a trading plan with strict entry and exit rules, employ risk management and money management strategies, and never average down into a losing position. Take profits and wait patiently, nice and relaxed, until the time comes to get back into the market. Trade actively when market conditions suit your trading style, and sit on your hands and do nothing when they are not aligned. There will be times when you simply should not be in the market.

Learn and prosper

Avoiding the mistake of averaging down — and all the other mistakes mentioned in this book — requires education. It is important to educate yourself about all aspects of the markets and the trading style you will employ. It is simply not good enough to make judgement calls based on a media story or the advice of a broker or other adviser. Education coupled with a disciplined and consistent approach to your trading will greatly enhance your ability to operate in a methodical, independent manner. Taking responsibility for your trading and investing decisions and actions will lift you beyond the realm of punter and have you well on the way to taking a professional and businesslike approach to your trading.

> The three key words are education, education and education. Then follow this through with discipline and a clear, methodical approach. Accept responsibility for your actions both in trading and in life. Become your own master and don't blame others for your mistakes and actions.

Tom Scollon is an economist who has worked in international trading with BHP, and in a number of managing director and chairman roles specialising in IT and finance. He is an active investor in many asset classes with considerable experience in equities, options and other derivatives in world markets. In this chapter, Tom told us about the dangers of averaging down when trading shares.

Tom is a sought-after speaker at a wide range of investment events. He is Chief Analyst for *SharesBulletin* <www.sharesbulletin.com.au>, Chief Editor of the online newsletter 'Trading Tutors', a contributor to *Money Magazine*, a columnist for *YourTradingEdge*, author of *Fair Share* and *Surfing the Market Waves*, and is guest commentator on radio and TV. He is a shareholder and director of Hubb (<www.hubb.com.au>).

I'm right! The market's wrong

Mistake 16: lacking discipline

Discipline is the bridge between goals and accomplishments.

Jim Rohn

The need for a consistent, disciplined and patient approach to trading is paramount to success in this business. A great deal of self-discipline is required to ensure that you consistently engage the markets according to the rules of your system or trading plan, even in the tough times when the system is in a drawdown or out of whack with the market. It is during these times that one's abilities as a trader are put to the test. The temptations to ignore signals or to randomly increase or decrease position sizing or, worse still, randomly execute trades based on 'gut feel' must be ignored. It is when the chips are down that the rules of your system as detailed in your trading plan must be adhered to meticulously. Avoiding the temptation to meddle with the strategy is a must.

Those with a thorough understanding of the range of probabilities and outcomes of their chosen strategy will be well prepared for these times. They will expect them and accept them as part and parcel of their trading operation. Those who are unprepared will be buffeted from pillar to post mentally and financially. People are attracted to trading to make money or by the challenge of wanting to succeed. However, those who have thought beyond this and who have done their homework before they enter their first trade will be way more prepared than those who simply rock along to a seminar, buy a book or two, or buy a trading system off the internet and think they are about to make their fortune trading.

It's not only about the money

Leading market psychologist and author Dr Harry Stanton shares his views on the need for clearly defined goals and a reason beyond just making money to provide structure and discipline in our trading endeavours:

> It is important to identify why you want to trade. The often quoted saying 'unless you know where you want to go you will end up somewhere else' is important to remember. I reckon if you asked 100 people why they are trading, 75 would say they just want to make money. Not many people look beyond this. Those who are trading and making money, which is reasonably rare, are usually quite happy. It's the ones who aren't making money or aren't being as successful as they thought they could be that begin having issues. These guys usually lack goals other than the one of 'making money'. The smarter ones will work out quite quickly that they are not going to succeed and give it away. However, the vast majority will not accept what they see in front of them. They will continue losing, adding money to their trading accounts, losing again, adding more money to their accounts, in a downward spiral. It just doesn't dawn on them that they are not in tune with making money in the markets.

One day at a time

> Some people are just never going to 'get' trading. For a variety of reasons they lack both the discipline and the desire to change. As I get older, I'm becoming increasingly cynical about people's

ability to change even when it is glaringly obvious that big changes are needed. In my practice I use techniques that are very effective in getting people to change — as long as this is what they want to do. The big problem in trading, and in life in general, is that people tend to think in ways that harm rather than ways that help. This is often referred to as self-sabotaging behaviour. People in general, and traders in particular, need to think in terms of living one day at a time. When you wake up in the morning, consider it a brand new start — be grateful. Mentally dump all the stuff you don't want in your life, keep what you do want and get on with it. Consider each trade as the first of one thousand trades you are going to make. Each trade is a fresh start. Look at each trade in this way, despite what happened in the last trade. Forget what happened last time, be disciplined and take today's trades regardless of the outcomes from yesterday.

It is also important to stop worrying about the future. Almost all the things we worry about never happen anyway! The outcome of the trade we take will not be influenced by worrying about it — it will just be. As traders, it is important to live in the present. Having the self-discipline to do this is very difficult for the majority of people.

Ego *is* a dirty word

Many people either make the transition to trading or begin trading on a part-time basis with expectations of success. They may be very successful in business or in their career (or have been in the past), and have managed to reach high levels in their chosen field of endeavour. With this comes an ego-driven desire to win and succeed as they have done in the past. Many would-be traders find it exceedingly difficult to accept losing. Yet — as discussed by Davin Clarke in chapter 7 and many other interviewees in this book — accepting losing trades is part and parcel of trading. Only by continually probing the market and accepting small losing trades are we able to then participate in the winning trades when they come along. Trading is not about being right. It is about managing losses. People's egos and the need to be right get in the way when they venture into the trading world. It is this ego that must be managed when trading.

> One of the things I have had to do with some people is convince them that trading isn't really what they should be doing. A lot of successful businesspeople think they have a point to prove. They want to master it at any cost. Winning and being right becomes more important than making money — they want to prove they can beat the market. They will keep going and lose a hell of a lot of money because of their ego. It is very difficult to ever get this ego out of the way for some people. These are the ones who really need to stop and re-assess what they are doing.

When the rubber hits the road

It is theoretically possible to learn about every aspect of trading from books, courses, gurus and market educators. It is not possible to learn theoretically how you will react in real time, when the rubber hits the road. This is when your money and ego are on the line and the decisions you make will affect what happens next. How you will react in good times and in bad can only be discovered through experience. This is when the concepts in your trading plan will be tested, as will your discipline to be able to perform under pressure. In these situations it is then important to have someone to turn to for help and guidance — someone who can help you learn from the experience so you can handle it better next time.

> It is very hard to train people how to theoretically handle a problem they haven't felt yet. Trading is very experiential. When people experience a certain problem or issue they need help in handling it at the time. You need to experience the problem and then work on how to solve it. It is difficult to solve problems in theory. Of course, the issue with trading is that these problems (mistakes) usually cost money and this raises emotional and psychological issues. Traders who are successful, have a system and understand money management tend to suffer fewer emotional and psychological issues than the ego-driven trader without a structured approach to trading. Trading is a

very disciplined activity. You can talk to people about emotional discipline till the cows come home, but they have to experience it to really grasp what it means.

Mindfulness

Experienced traders are well aware of the importance of managing their trading psychology. Through keeping their ego in check and working on understanding how they react under pressure and handle their own thought processes, they are able to reach a point of emotional detachment from the outcome of their trades. Much of this can be attributed to the application of a robust trading system with a clearly defined 'edge' and money management techniques coupled with the ability to practise mindfulness—watching and monitoring their own thoughts.

> Those who are able to achieve this state of mindfulness become separated from the actual processes of analysing the markets and trading. It is almost as if they are totally uninvolved and detached from the process. They are able to virtually watch themselves trade and observe their emotions and reactions to what is happening. They are able to watch themselves from an external locus, performing the trading activities but remaining detached at an emotional level. Very few people can achieve this state consistently.

Watching you, watching who?

Despite the urgings and encouragement of many that trading can be taught to everyone (which it can in theory), not everyone will be suited to the rigorous mental activity and high levels of self-discipline required when actively trading. Sure, everyone can learn how to do it, but not all will have the discipline and continued desire to apply themselves to the markets consistently over time. Equally important as learning how to trade is knowing when to stop trading if it is not working out.

Some people just aren't suited to trading and, despite all their efforts, won't make a success of it. In these cases they can tend to place too much emphasis on psychological issues in an attempt to justify 'why' they aren't suited to trading. They tend to seek help to discover why they can't be successful traders, or why they are the way they are. This in itself is ridiculous because we never really get an answer when we ask 'why?' While it is sensible to examine trading results and determine success or otherwise from a mathematical and statistical perspective, delving back into the deep dark past in an attempt to come up with a reason 'why' we are not successful has fairly limited application. You may be doing all the right things according to the so-called trading experts and still be losing money. The fact is, you are just not suited to it, and you have to accept that. In the words of the French playwright Molière, 'Things are worth what we make them worth'.

Adopting a disciplined approach

The majority of these issues arise from a discretionary or arbitrary approach to trading. Poring over charts, conducting detailed analysis and agonising over entry and exit signals is the undoing of most traders. The need to be right, ego issues, fear, greed, uncertainty and every other emotion begin to interfere in some way or another with traders' decision-making processes as they attempt to guess what the market will do next. Add to this, stories in the media, use of a mix–match of indicators and theories, and a lack of awareness of how markets work, and the trader is doomed to a life of trading misery. However, all is not lost! Mechanical trading systems (see chapter 17) can provide traders with a way to be involved in the markets without the need to agonise over trading decisions. As long as they are disciplined in the application of the rules of the system, much of the personal angst associated with independently trading can be reduced or eliminated.

What the vast majority of people must do is to have a totally mechanical system that cuts out this second-guessing — one that allows them to execute trades according to the rules of the system without having to think, 'should I get in here, should I get out here?' If they are able to do it without thinking about it, this cuts out a lot of the angst and emotional turmoil. It also helps them achieve the emotional discipline needed to trade with any reasonable degree of success. Mechanical traders avoid the emotional swings experienced by more subjective traders. The virtue of a good mechanical system is how it defines where you are and what you are doing at all times. The traders who are well disciplined in their trading and in their lives will typically be using a mechanical system of some sort. They are able to manage their moods and emotions and are consistent in their approach to the markets. A mechanical system neutralises the lack of self-discipline that the vast majority of people seem to have.

In an 'experiment' conducted a few years ago, a trading educator provided seminar attendees with a mechanical trading system that had been profitable in 18 of the past 20 years. A journalist was one of the attendees. His job was to interview each of the traders after 12 months. At the end of the 12 months only one of the 117 attendees was still trading the system in its original form. Several gave up after the first few losing trades, others tweaked it or changed it, and others started improvising trades on the back of the system. Only one had the self-discipline to consistently implement the system as it was designed. He made money.

Dr Harry Stanton is a Fellow of the Australian Society of Hypnosis, a Fellow of the American Society of Clinical Hypnosis, and a Member of the Australian Psychological Society. He has had over 30 years' experience in the practice of clinical psychology and hypnotherapy, writing extensively on these subjects in academic journals. In this chapter, Harry explained the psychology behind successful (and unsuccessful) trading behaviour.

Dr Stanton is a consultant on the application of psychology to a wide range of practical activities. The basis of his work is self-empowerment, morale building and performance enhancement, helping people to manage their lives more successfully by overcoming the obstacles they create within their own minds. Dr Stanton is frequently consulted by the business community on how they might apply psychological principles to improve performance. In addition to keynoting conferences, he conducts workshops, both internationally and in Australia, on confidence-building, the psychology of investing and trading, self-motivation, motivating others, the effective use of time, persuasive communication, problem solving, decision making, coping with stress and managing people. He has authored over 250 articles and nine books including the popular *Let the Trade Wins Flow: psychology for super traders.*

The emotions of a robot

Mistake 17: emotive and subjective trading

There is nothing either good or bad, but thinking makes it so.

William Shakespeare

Developing the skill set required for implementing a mechanical trading system or strategy is the only way to achieve consistent and continued success as a trader. The old saying of 'never mistake brains for a bull market' has proved time and again to be one of the most pertinent comments ever made in relation to trading. During times of extended bullish euphoria in any market, when prices appear to be in a never-ending uptrend, complacency and poor decision-making processes creep in as small mistakes and indiscretions are quickly covered up by the rising tide. However, these mistakes can prove much more costly—both financially and psychologically—when markets turn or during extended range trading periods.

My two favourite trading subjects are money management and mechanical trading. Ryan Jones is the mentor who taught me about the importance of money management, so I have left him to explain this topic in chapter 8. My interest in trading mechanically began years ago in the early stages of my trading business. I would observe myself become emotionally involved in trades, either good or bad, and making subjective decisions caused by emotion and lack of discipline. Man, what a roller-coaster ride! In my role as a trader coach I still see these same issues repeated over and over again by all levels of traders and investors.

I remember having written naked call options in RIO for which I had received about $5000 premium, believing the stock to be in a downtrend. Unfortunately for me though, the market thought otherwise. A quick rebound in the price of RIO saw this particular trade turn into a $20 000 loser—a decent hit! I spent a few days agonising over the loss, but once I recovered I vowed to completely eliminate the use of any discretionary decisions in my trading.

I knew there had to be a 'better' way—a way that would allow me to develop and discover systems that had a high probability of success and then to implement the trades without attachment to the outcome. This for me was mechanical trading, either through auto-execution systems on the futures markets, or robust strategies for the equity markets with clearly defined entry, exit and position sizing rules. The implementation of these auto-trade programs has been significantly enhanced by the services of John Robertson at <www.i-deal.com.au> (see chapter 19).

Consistently inconsistent

Many of these mistakes can be attributed to arbitrary and subjective decision-making processes loosely based on 'gut feel', moon phases, tips from mates and brokers, the latest and greatest magical indicator, or whatever else seems appealing at the time. Traders using such an approach, with no clearly defined set of rules for market engagement are constantly chopping and changing their trade entry and exit rules as well as their position sizes and risk tolerance with absolutely no consistency in their decision-making processes. Their whole strategy is virtually a random series of events—some that work and some that don't—with most winning trades attributed to good luck rather than any particular level of skill or ability as a trader. One trade entry will be based on an indicator crossover, while the next will be based on a chart pattern, and the next on a bit of 'insider information'.

Much more dangerous, however, will be the random methods by which trades are exited.

While trading in this way may appear to work for a short period of time or during a specific set of market conditions, over the long term it is doomed to fail, not only because market conditions will change, as they always do, but also because the demands on the trader to continue to engage the markets in this way are time consuming, stressful and all-encompassing. Discretionary trading requires the trader to be constantly in contact with the market, constantly monitoring any number of chart patterns, indicators, phases, count-back levels, and whatever combination of methods they are using to somehow arrive at their entry and exit decisions. This is mentally and emotionally exhausting.

Decisions made for a trade that 'works' and returns a profit result in feelings of euphoria and happiness. When the same decisions result in a losing trade, feelings of frustration and anger occur. The trader then uses a completely different combination of indicators and information to arrive at the next decision, and the same feelings and emotions are experienced all over again. The psychological impact of this style of trading is negative and stressful in the extreme. There is a huge amount of pressure on the trader to continue to make decisions and they are constantly 'busy' as they jump around from method to method. More often than not, the whole exercise ends with the trader imploding financially, or withdrawing from the markets as they are unable to cope with the rigorous demands of the trading environment they have created for themselves.

Underperformance

While it is possible to achieve a decent rate of return when trading in a discretionary manner during a specific set of market conditions, it will not deliver consistent outperformance over the long term. Discretionary traders usually achieve their best results during bull markets and extended uptrends, and tend to fall into the trap of believing that, first, the uptrend will continue, second, that they will continue to profit from their strategy, and, third, that trading is easy. In trading terms they are referred to as 'mistaking brains for a bull market'. When the market conditions change, their 'trading' ability comes under pressure, the number of losses increase, and they are eventually wiped out or stop trading. At best, they significantly underperform the market.

The major issue that tends to be avoided by these traders is position sizing and money management. Little heed is paid to risk management, usually because these traders have little or no understanding of these concepts. Nor do they comprehend the devastating results that can occur from over-leveraged accounts, over trading and excessive position sizes. Position sizing strategies are ignored as these inexperienced traders jostle to get as a big a slice of the action as they can, believing the next trade will be their ticket to owning their own island paradise in a South Pacific tax haven. For a while they get away with it and some easy profits are made. Then, inevitably, the market changes direction—usually quickly, as there are simply no buyers left, and no more 'greater fools' willing to keep buying overpriced shares, futures contracts, Forex spreads or any other instrument. These major corrections, or crashes, are then attributed to some external source and the blame game begins! It is now 'someone else's' fault that prices are falling and companies are collapsing under mountains of debt, dodgy loan deals or whatever other story is doing the rounds. These same traders who were so keen to expound their successes and new-found ability to pick market direction are now licking their wounds and denouncing the markets as a place for 'insiders' who all knew the market was about to collapse and 'made' them buy at high prices.

Do you see what I see?

A big problem when trading on a discretionary or subjective basis is the interpretation of data and information. As humans, we all 'see' the world differently. What appears as something to one person can appear completely different to another. Where one trader identifies divergence, another doesn't. Where one sees a third wave up in a five-stage downtrend, another sees the final leg down before the beginning of an uptrend. One trader's interpretation of a combination of factors and indicators can vary drastically from that of another. These traders also tend to be highly influenced by the news, views and opinions of others (see chapter 14). They may convince themselves that they will exit a position with a 'mental' trailing stop, without actually placing the stop order in the market. They tell themselves that if the stop price is reached, they will place the order. When the price does fall to their 'stop' level, they hear some good news that relates to their position and decide to stay in the trade in the belief that the price will rise again on the basis of this news or some other analyst's view. When the price falls even further, they either exit in frustration at a much lower price, or add another 'investment' to their portfolio.

Mechanical trading aims to eliminate these subjective decisions and replace them with an objective and disciplined approach. Mechanical trading systems can range from highly developed mathematical algorithms that auto-execute trades from a live trading platform, to using chart-based patterns or simple indicator crosses and other triggers to enter and exit trades. Whatever method is used, it can only be considered a 'system' if a strict set of rules or conditions exists, and entries and exits are taken consistently and constantly, without rationalising the trade. The thinking stage needs to occur during the development of the system. Once it is developed, tested and fully understood, then it must be simply applied to the market and adhered to 100 per cent of the time. This is obviously much easier when using a fully automated system that sends orders electronically to the market without the trader having to actually manually place the order. If it is a system or a market that requires the trader to place the orders manually, via a trading platform or a phone call to the broker, then these must be placed every time, regardless of any thoughts the trader may have as to the appropriateness of the trade.

Picking fruit

When using a mechanical system, it is important to avoid attempting to 'cherry pick' trades. This term is used to describe the temptation to attempt to pick the 'best' trades and bypass those trades considered to be irrelevant. This almost always ends in disaster as personal bias will influence the decisions and result in the trades taken actually bearing no correlation with the overall results of the system. It is a common mistake made by many new system traders, and usually unfolds along these lines:

Example 1

After deciding to purchase and trade a mechanical system, Joan experienced a few losing trades, leading to a bit of frustration and anxiety. The next trade started well and began to show some decent profit. The price then started to move against the position and some of the profit began to erode. Frustrated by the first few losses and watching this position give back some of the early profit, Joan decided to override the system and close out the position for a small profit. The trade then turned around and continued in the original direction and went on to make a large profit which made up for these few losing trades and pushed the system to new equity highs but without Joan involved in the trade. She then participated in the next few trades, which also turned out to be small losses. Out of frustration she gave up trading the system just as it hit a winning streak of five trades in a row. Following this winning run, with the system now having proven itself again, Joan decided to follow the signals again, only to experience a couple of losses, and the whole cycle repeated itself.

A client of mine began trading a mechanical trading system with impressive results over the long term. In the first few months the system did well and Justin's account grew by around 25 per cent. The system then went into a drawdown, and gave back over half the profit that had been made. Frustrated, Justin elected to stop trading the system for a while to 'wait and see what happens'. Over the next three weeks the system hit a fantastic winning streak and returned in excess of 30 per cent for that month. Justin missed out on this profit and turned the system on again when it reached new equity highs. The system again went into drawdown. However, this time

Justin stuck with the system, lived through the drawdown and has watched his equity curve improve substantially.

The real trick to mechanical trading or trading a system is to buy or develop one that suits your personality and trading style. There is little point attempting to trade an aggressive short-term system that generates frequent signals if you are more relaxed and looking to capture long-term trends. It is also important not to over-optimise a system, so that it appears on paper and from back-testing to be the perfect answer to all your trading requirements. This is a process known as 'curve-fitting', where the system is built to fit the existing historical data. Invariably, these systems will fail once live trading commences.

Managing the system

The only 'interference' that need occur when trading a mechanical system is managing the system during periods of extreme drawdown. All systems will experience periods when they suffer a string of losing trades. Some will be greater than others depending on the style of the system and the money management rules being employed within the system. One way to manage these periods of drawdown is to apply a moving average to the equity curve of the system's results, and use this as a switch to turn the system on and off. When the equity curve dips below the moving average as it goes into drawdown the system is turned off. The signals to trade are not taken until the equity curve of profit crosses back above the moving average. The aim is to minimise the amount of profit given back during these drawdowns. Figure 17.1 (overleaf) shows the equity curve of a mechanical trading system as the top line. The bottom line is the moving average of this equity curve. It is easy to see from the chart the periods when the equity curve is above the moving average allowing the signals to be traded. Similarly, the periods when the equity curve is below the moving average and the system would be turned off and not traded can also be seen.

Figure 17.1: system equity curve with moving average

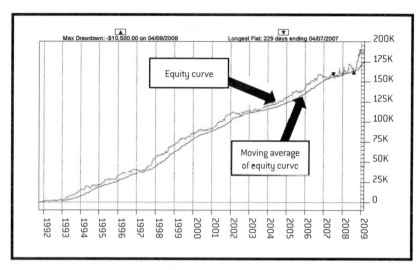

Source: Trade Navigator © Genesis Financial Technologies, Inc.

Understanding drawdowns

Trading systems, regardless of the market in which they operate, will always experience equity drawdowns. If a system wins 60 per cent of the time, then it is only logical that 40 per cent of the time it won't be making new equity highs, and will theoretically be in drawdown. It is the management of these drawdowns and how they are handled psychologically that is important.

Futures market traders are, by nature of the markets in which they trade, much more aligned to an acceptance of equity drawdowns than are the majority of equity traders. This arises for three main reasons:

1. Futures positions are not normally considered to be long-term 'buy and hold' type investments. Thus, they are more suited to systems with predefined entry and exit strategies.

2. Futures markets tend to lack the emotional attachment that is created by stock markets. Given the high level of involvement in equity markets by a wider cross-section of

the trading and investing community (either directly or indirectly through their superannuation and retirement fund accounts), emotions tend to run high in these markets. As a result, people's expectations and emotions can wreak havoc with the decision-making processes required to exit losing trades and take profit on winning trades.

3. Far more futures traders trade with mechanical systems than equity traders. Mechanical traders expect drawdown as a natural part of their trading because they trained to think in terms of probabilities rather than overemphasising the importance of individual trades.

Experienced traders expect that systems will go into drawdown as a result of them being out of sync with the direction of the market for periods of time. Overall though, if the system is solid, has well-researched entry and exit rules, and strict money management rules that provide an edge, it will be in sync with the market enough to be profitable over the long term.

Timing can be an issue when initially deploying any trading system. If the system hits a winning streak when first turned on, then any subsequent drawdowns will be from profits. However, chances are that you will experience the drawdown when the system is first used. In this case, the drawdown will be from initial capital. If you are unprepared for this mentally and financially and have not fully researched or do not fully understand the system, you will be frustrated and angry and begin to doubt the system. This often leads to the trader ceasing trading the system and moving to another, which also goes into an immediate drawdown. The cycle is repeated, creating a lifelong cycle of inconsistency. Preparation, a thorough understanding of the range of probabilities of the system, and an adequate level of capital to sustain you through these potential immediate drawdowns is essential.

To achieve the consistency offered by mechanical trading requires the development of a trader's mindset and the patience and discipline to stick with the system. By doing this you will participate in the profitable trades and the gradual rise in total equity that will occur over the long term.

The key to success when trading is not so much what you make when your system is generating profits, but how you mange it (and yourself) when it is not!

A trader's mindset

Consistent traders have learned to think in terms of probabilities and the long-term performance and returns of their trading system delivered as a result of its 'edge'. The outcome of individual trades loses relevance and is replaced with an understanding that winning trades, losing trades, drawdowns and new equity highs are all just the probabilities of the system playing out in real time. They are 'normal' occurrences that the trader accepts and has trained for. They actually expect them to happen and are able to deal with the range of outcomes that can occur through studying and understanding both the system they are trading and, most importantly, themselves.

These probabilities are determined by the number of winners versus the number of losers and, more importantly, the size of the average win compared to the size of the average loss over a large sample size. These numbers will also include the size of the largest loss, the size of the largest win, largest drawdown, longest winning streak, longest losing streak and all other variables and outcomes that the system is capable of. When these numbers are measured over a large trade sample across varying market conditions, then you can determine the range of probable outcomes for the system. Anything other than this is gambling.

The importance of testing a system over a large sample size is critical. Too often, beginner traders and system developers draw rash and inconclusive results from a small sample of trades and brief experiences. Craving instant success and gratification, they launch into trading a system that has been designed and tested during a specific set of market conditions, only to find that when these conditions change, the system implodes. It is far better to spend time researching and testing the system over a large sample of data before employing it in real time. The patient system developer and system trader will develop a level of empathy with the market that will be justly rewarded over the long term. This empathy means that they no longer think in terms of the relevance of individual trade outcomes, but that they fully expect, accept and embrace the range of probabilities that the system can deliver. They have also learnt to expect the unexpected, knowing that at some time in the future the system will experience its largest win, largest loss, and every other variable. Traders who dismiss market empathy and understanding as unimportant are destined to failure.

What colour is your box?

Mechanical trading or trading a well-developed and researched system should not be confused with 'black box' systems. Black box systems offer you the 'latest market secret' or exciting new indicator that has never been offered to the public before. They are usually a hoax. They are the epitome of curve-fitted systems that appear to give amazing results. Unfortunately for the unsuspecting purchaser, they have been designed and tested to 'fit' a given set of market conditions. Once the market conditions change, and the specific set of variables that are 'unique to this system' change, then the black box system will implode, often with quite dramatic results.

A well-researched, developed and tested mechanical trading system that has proven results over varying market conditions enables the trader to engage the market consistently in a disciplined and businesslike fashion. It will eliminate the emotional turmoil and extended decision-making processes experienced by the majority of discretionary traders and those with no real plan for interacting with the market. Mechanical trading systems streamline the whole trading process and reduce the mental and emotional anguish often experienced by more subjective traders.

Overworked and underpaid

Mistake 18: overtrading

Nothing is really work unless you would rather be doing something else.

James Matthew Barrie

A common refrain among everyone involved in trading is 'don't overtrade'. But overtrading can be hard to define. How do we know when we are trading too much versus not enough? What one trader may consider overtrading, another may consider just a normal day's or week's work. An active short-term trader may trade in and out of the market several times a day. An active medium-term trader may trade several times a month. The trader with the medium-term approach may consider the short-term guy to be overtrading, while the short-term trader may think the medium-term dude isn't trading enough!

We need to define what overtrading means to each of us in line with our trading plan, and the time and capital we have available to trade with. This will also be influenced by our personality and trading style. Short-term traders with high energy levels and an ability to retain an intense level of concentration during market hours will obviously place way more trades than the more relaxed medium-term trader content to avoid the intraday noise of the market and place trades based on end-of-day scans and entry rules. Those holding down day jobs or running a business and unable to participate in the daily market action will also be trading longer time frames than those with the time and resources to be able to actively day or short-term trade. For these people, mechanical trading systems and even auto-execution systems (both discussed in chapter 17) are definitely advantageous.

Too much or not too much — is that the question?

Given that any definition of overtrading will be imprecise and influenced by many factors, I asked some of the interviewees for this book to define overtrading.

Jake Bernstein

Overtrading is a relative term. Clearly the term is in the eye of the beholder. What is overtrading to one individual may well be 'undertrading' to another. That being said, there must be some external basis of comparison or definition. Here are several guidelines that I would suggest:

1. Are you making money? If you are making money then the odds are that you aren't overtrading. Several years ago I was an expert witness in a law case involving an individual who was making up to 600 day trades daily. Was that overtrading? He was making big money. By my standards it was overtrading, but given that he was making a great deal of money it wasn't overtrading by his definition. Of course, when he started losing money other traders looked at the volume of his trading and decided that he was definitely overtrading.

2. Is the game worth playing? In other words, is there enough money being made to justify the intensity of

the effort being expended? For example, if a trader needs to spend 14 hours a day intensely involved in trading in order to make a few hundred dollars then I would say that he or she is overtrading. It's a good idea to figure out your earnings per hour. Could you be making as much money per hour working at McDonald's?

3. Are you making more than the broker? This one speaks for itself.

4. What are the physical, emotional and relationship costs of your trading? If any or all of these important areas of your life are suffering or being stretched, you are overtrading.

Ryan Jones

Overtrading is anytime you are risking too much either for your own comfort level to stick with the trade and/or strategy, or when an expected drawdown would render the account unable to trade through the drawdown. Often times, traders severely underestimate their ability to deal with risk. I have talked repeatedly with traders who say one thing, but when the rubber hits the road, they do another. They say they can handle a $10000 drawdown and continue trading, but when the drawdown hits $8000, they are looking for a clean pair of shorts. This is where most of the mistakes are made in trading, and they almost always lead to disaster.

It is a very common mistake for traders to push the limits with the expected drawdown as well. For example, let's say you analyse a trading system and determine that the largest expected drawdown is around $10000. It is foolish to start trading with a $10000 account, or $12000, or even $15000 in this situation. In fact, I suggest 2.5 times the expected drawdown size as the absolute minimum starting account. Even this may be pushing it, depending on how well the system was analysed. Largest expected drawdowns will almost always exceed those limits in real trading, and you have to not only be willing to hit them, but trade through them to some predetermined stopping point if the drawdown continues. This takes tremendous discipline and preparation.

Larry Williams

I think there two types of overtrading: trading too many times; and having too many on. In other words, one person may be trading, say, 15 times a week and that is overtrading. Another person may only trade once a month but is still overtrading because his position size is way too big for his account.

In either case the trader has so many balls bouncing in the air that he cannot focus on what he should be doing; there are too many distractions.

Errors, instability and dirty laundry

Though it may be a relative term, the negative impacts of overtrading are the same regardless of your trading system, time frame or account size. Overtrading through frustration or attempting to prove that you are right, over-excitement at all the potential trading opportunities you see, or any other reason, needs to be identified early. This will allow you to stop and reassess what is causing you to overtrade. Some of the tell-tale signs of overtrading are discussed below.

Jake Bernstein

Not necessarily in order of importance:

1. Is your health suffering? Do you have high stress, high blood pressure or other symptoms?

2. Is your psychological health deteriorating?

3. Are your interpersonal relationships suffering by virtue of the time spent on trading?

4. Is your error rate increasing due to the large number of trades you are making?

Consider this: if a trader has a fully automatic system that enters orders and tracks positions automatically and trades 600 times a day and it makes money, is that considered overtrading? Unless it loses money, I say no.

Ryan Jones

If you wake up one morning, take a peek at your account balance and then need to go find a clean pair of shorts then you are probably overtrading. Of course, I'm being sarcastic here, but experienced traders know exactly the feeling I am talking about. Do not ignore your gut feelings about a situation. If you are continually nervous in a drawdown, mistakes are soon to follow. This is only the psychological side of it. Overtrading can be a matter of fact, not just feeling. Unfortunately, tell-tale signs of overtrading as a matter of fact and not just feeling are very difficult to detect until it is too late. However, careful analysis prior to trading can dramatically reduce the probability of actually overtrading. If you merely glance at some stats, grow dollar signs for eyeballs and just start trading without seriously looking at the risks, the probabilities of hitting those risks and understanding what type of market conditions might contribute more to realising the risks, you tremendously increase the probability of overtrading.

(Matter of fact overtrading is when the starting account size is not big enough to more than handle the expected drawdown without forcing the trader to add more funds or stop trading the strategy altogether.)

Dr Harry Stanton

The best indicator of overtrading is changes to your sleep patterns and/or not sleeping at night. This occurs as a result of increased anxiety, fear and worry.

John Robertson

> Amending stops is a sure sign of someone overtrading. In the floor trading days we used to call it 'GTT': Good Till Threatened. These traders move their stops, hoping to avoid the loss because they can't afford another losing trade. They are always hoping the next trade will be a big winner. Invariably they keep losing.

A line in the sand

There is obviously a big distinction to be made between overtrading and actively trading an account to maximise profit potential from the system being traded. The scalper trading 600 times per day may or may not be overtrading; just as the medium-term trader executing six trades per week may or may not be overtrading. The line in the sand is money management and position sizing (discussed in chapter 8) and running your trading operation in a professional and businesslike manner.

Brett Steenbarger

> If traders keep statistics on their trading (which I strongly recommend), they can calculate the average number of trades and shares/round turns traded per day. This allows them to identify days in which they trade more and less actively than usual. The key is comparing this relative trading activity with the actual opportunity afforded by the market. For example, if you see that the market traded in a narrow range on slow volume, but that you were trading more actively than usual, that's a good sign that frustration might have been leading to overtrading.

Justine Pollard

> Actively trading an account to maximise returns is all about risk management. Instead of continuing to take on more positions, you are best to focus on adding to positions that are already profitable by pyramiding and other position sizing techniques.

This ensures you maximise your returns on the successful trades.

Money can only be made by large profits and small losses. Unfortunately, we don't know which trades will be winners. Once trades start to move well and prove themselves you can then maximise the return by adding to them. Every new trade that is opened has the potential to be a loss. Amateur traders tend to be more interested in entering more trades than adding to existing winning trades. Instead, they take more losses rather than adding to their profitable trades and building on these.

The reality is that it will only be a few trades that make you the big money and you want to hit these trades hard and maximise on them.

Ryan Jones

The key to maximising returns is to have a well-thought-out trading plan in place before you start trading. This trading plan should include a blunt analysis of the strategy (or strategies) being traded and the risks associated with them. It should detail the exact equity levels at which trade size will either increase or decrease, and the trader needs to fully understand the ramifications of those decisions. Money management is not something that traders can approach lightly. Serious traders who are not simply trying to stroke their egos or get rich quick will take the time to understand the whole concept of money management in trading. If you don't understand money management concepts, then you are taking a shot in the dark and this will often lead to overtrading.

Who are you?

Overtrading and its consequences can be linked to the old adversaries of fear and greed which cause irrational, illogical behaviour if not recognised and fully understood. Those with a well-developed understanding of themselves and the markets and a well-developed plan for engaging the markets will be less inclined to suffer the negative effects of overtrading than those with a reckless 'gung-ho' approach to their trading.

Larry Williams

I'm certain that the higher the anxiety level of a person, the more trades they will be putting on. Also the newer one is to this business the more one will be trading. Most traders who are overtrading are trying to make a fortune in a hurry which, unfortunately, often means they are trying to catch up and make money back. The only way they think that can be done is to take large positions and/or trade way too often.

I think this is also a sign that one does not have a systematic approach to the market.

Dr Harry Stanton

There are two sides to the coin:

1. There are those who are totally overconfident and ego-driven. They are convinced they are right and the market is wrong and all they have to do is 'keep going' and they will eventually prove that they are right. They continue to throw more and more money at the markets until they are eventually proven wrong when they have no money left with which to trade.

2. On the other hand are those who are very fearful. They lose money and think they have to make it back. They bet more and more on each trade until they eventually blow up or they spend endless hours finding a 'sure thing' trade that they believe cannot lose. They then take a massive position in the trade, and it loses!

Justine Pollard

Amateur traders tend to overtrade as they are new to trading and their need to be in the market and fear of missing out is at its strongest level. I know I was there once too and I know how easy it is to overtrade and wanting to be in everything. It takes time to realise that this is not the most effective way to trade and the quickest way to burn your trading capital.

It is also easy to overtrade when you have had a good run of profits and think that you are invincible and the more you trade the more you make. The market will soon show you this is not the case and your ego has become larger. It will bring your ego back down to earth again.

Ryan Jones

I believe that everyone who gets involved in trading must fight greed and personality flaws. I have never met a perfect trader, and never will. I don't believe ability has anything to do with it. I truly believe that anyone who is determined to be successful can be, with enough preparation. I also believe that no matter what the personality, determination can overcome. Having said that, there are some personality types that suffer severe stress when taking risks. Traders need to consider the consequences of putting themselves under that kind of stress. If the stress affects your health, or your relationships, or your overall demeanour, I would seriously consider not trading at all. I actually told a trader one time that he simply was not cut out to trade. He became irate with me, but it was the truth. The potential benefits simply were not worth the costs.

Getting it right

The overtrading trap can be avoided by having realistic money-making objectives, performance measures and personal goals for your trading. The trading arena provides us with an endless array of opportunities across a wide range of markets virtually 24 hours per day, six-and-a-half days per week. It is easy to be sucked into this vortex—not only trading in your own daytime hours, but late into the night or in the early mornings as you attempt to participate in market moves on a virtually never-ending basis. The results on your physical and mental health are costly, not to mention the destruction of your social life and the weird persona you take on after having been glued to a computer screen (or screens) for hours and hours. The use of automated trading systems and execution platforms will help alleviate this issue, as they allow your system to trade without you having to sit and watch the screen all day and night. The need for a disciplined approach (see chapter 16), a trading plan (see chapter 3), money management strategies (see chapter 8) and a definite 'edge' (see chapter 10) to your trading will help ensure you are not eaten by the overtrading monster.

Brett Steenbarger

In basic terms, overtrading refers to the placing of impulsive trades that are outside of one's plans and trading strengths. Much of this overtrading occurs because of anger and frustration, particularly following losses. By creating and using a checklist of what they need to see in a set-up prior to placing a trade, traders can exercise greater self-control and avoid overtrading. Taking short breaks during the trading day to relax and regain focus can also be helpful in reducing frustration and impulsive trading. Trading actively with a demonstrated edge is not overtrading; it's when we trade on impulse, without an edge, that we 'overtrade'.

Larry Williams

I think the best way to eliminate these problems is to say you cannot have more than 'x' exposure on your account. Let's say you don't want to have more than 15 per cent of your account exposed to risk at any given time. That, through a variety of money management formulas, will tell you how many positions you should have and the size of those positions.

Justine Pollard

You must follow a strict trading plan that has money management rules focused on position sizing and portfolio heat management. It is one thing to have the plan; it is another to follow it. You also need a good record-keeping structure to ensure you know where you stand in the market at all times and do not trade beyond your allocated capital amount.

Ryan Jones

Know your risks and overprepare for them. The trading world is obsessed with market prediction. In my book, that is the evil 'P' word. I encourage all traders to replace their desire to predict market action with a determination to properly prepare for the adventure. Prediction is overrated. Preparation is king.

Fat fingers, 10 000 too many and busting trades

Mistake 19: operational errors

Mistakes are painful when they happen, but years later a collection of mistakes is what is called experience.

Dennis Waitley

With the growth in the use of online trading platforms allowing anyone with a computer and access to the internet to trade without the use of a traditional voice broker, the onus of responsibility for ensuring that all trade details are entered correctly sits squarely on the shoulders of the self-directed trader. Without the 'checking mechanism' of this third party, the online trader has to ensure that the correct quantity of shares or contracts is entered, at the correct price, in the chosen market, and that the correct directive to buy or sell is given. This can be further complicated by the use of more complex orders such as 'market if touched', 'stop and reverse', and orders with more than one 'leg'. These may include spread trades, or intermarket price action where a specific condition in one market causes an entry or exit signal in another market.

For the computer and tech-savvy trader, these issues may not be as important as they are to those with less skill or confidence in these areas. Nonetheless, mistakes can and do occur and they can happen to all of us regardless of our level of experience and operational skills. Even traditional voice brokers executing trades on behalf of clients can make these mistakes, so it is important to know how to deal with them and what to do in the event of a mistake occurring.

Who fears the executioner?

John Robertson from I-deal Financial Group, a boutique Australian-based broking firm specialising in the use of online trading platforms, acknowledges that the increased number of people now executing orders has led to an increase in the number of overall execution errors.

> The use of online trading platforms has increased the amount and frequency of errors. The more operators, the more execution errors. The reduction in training of these operators has also increased the amount of errors. Prior to the widespread use of electronic trading platforms, virtually all orders were executed in the trading pits or on the trading floor by highly trained brokers and operators. These days, anyone with a computer can execute their own orders, some with little or no training.
>
> Self-directed trading has reduced the execution risk for brokers with clients self-placing (filling) orders. Brokers, regulators and exchanges are being diligent through education to try to minimise this problem. Online traders must be aware of the extra responsibilities that they take on when they place live orders. Online platforms are not for everybody!
>
> Errors can range from the simple (clicking on buy instead of sell) to complex errors that are difficult to unwind. Money lost can wipe out the trading account. Errors can exist on any item that needs to be modified for the order to be placed.
>
> Errors such as placing a sell order instead of a buy order are just a mouse click away; it is very difficult for the online platform's automatic safety net to prevent these errors.
>
> Errors such as wrong prices are probably the most frequent. Fat fingers (typos) such as typing in to 'Buy 10 000' lots instead

of '1000' lots are easily made. Typing in the incorrect markets code (mnemonic) can lead to an error. Buying BHP in the USA instead of the ASX can occur on global platforms if not properly checked.

Very few errors are exited at a profit as, by definition, to exit immediately you must at minimum cross the spread of the market price; that is, sell the bid.

Not all these orders are filled immediately and many can be cancelled before they are filled in the market. For example, a limit order incorrectly put in below the market price will still be pending and give the operator time to amend before being filled.

Some orders placed too far from the market are recognised as errors by advances in technology which automatically reject the order. If you accidentally place a buy order way over the current market price as a limit order, the order will not go to market. Exchanges can 'bust' trades (cancel trades) if they believe they are out of market.

Redefining the role of the broker

The growth of online and self-directed trading has redefined the role of the broker from telephone order taker to a virtual electronic 'partner' in their client's trading business. In this regard brokers have an important role in knowing and understanding the trading platforms they are offering to their clients, and providing education and training in the operation of these platforms. Derivatives traders may need more than one online platform to cover the markets and instruments they are trading. In this circumstance the role of the broker in helping to educate traders in the use of these different platforms is very important.

> The emphasis on 'knowing the platform' and getting the client to be comfortable using it to participate in the market is now critical. This knowledge helps decrease the risk of errors.
>
> With the markets changing from the old open outcry pit-style trading to virtually 100 per cent electronic, brokers have

had to adapt or perish. To properly service clients with an online platform brokers must:

⇨ know the workings of their clients' platforms and the pros and cons of each of them

⇨ be IT literate—brokers need to know the installation and set-up of the platform and how to 'fix' them in the event of a malfunction. IT departments are of help, but the broker really needs to know it as well. This includes the platform's attributes for trading, charting, research and how it works through the computer

⇨ know the markets their clients are trading and have detailed knowledge of margin requirements, opening and closing times, liquidity issues and other market-specific information

⇨ understand their clients and their trading platforms

⇨ know where the clients' account information is—this is vital for risk management and to ensure proper money management rules are in place

⇨ know where the client's trade module is (orders) so they can oversee the orders and ensure the client has placed the correct orders. Knowing how and what the client trades assists greatly

⇨ set-up the trading conditions for clients so they have access to the markets they wish to trade. No use in missing trades at 3 am because the client has no trading rights or limits set-up for that market. Having trading limits and trading rights to particular markets can prevent the wrong market being accidentally traded and errors occurring

⇨ provide education on the markets, the platforms and trading in general. At a minimum, clients need confidence to place the orders through their knowledge of the platforms. Our platform, for example, has a demonstration available to practise on without firing off live orders into the market. This allows clients to gain confidence with the platform before trading with real money. Modern online platforms have in-built webinars to demonstrate the platform's functions to the client. This enables clients to personalise the platform to suit their preferences. We set-up the default version of our platforms so clients do not have to start from scratch.

One great advantage of online platforms is the ability to send financial news and research direct to the client in real time. This allows for an international research team to keep the online user up to date. Information, analysis and news are just a click away, enabling an informed investment decision. This can help reduce trade errors, and can be critical over financial data releases or unplanned international events.

Many clients are still finding that they really do need pro-fessional assistance to be successful in the markets. The easy access to global markets has not diminished the risks involved. Brokers who can provide more than a slick sales pitch and cheap brokerage rates are becoming highly prized. Cheap brokerage generated by ticking the 'no service' box is not always the best option for the trader looking for financial success.

Oh, #@%&! I pressed the wrong button!

Brokers and online platform providers spend a lot of time and effort minimising the chances of errors occurring. But we live in the real world where they can and do occur. One of the more common errors that all brokers see is that of keying in the wrong number of shares or contracts to buy or sell. This can be a simple 'fat finger' typo where the order is sent off as buying 10 000 instead of 1000 shares. If the trader's account has the funds available for this extra trade size, then the transaction will occur and the order will transact in the market.

If an incorrect quantity or code for a stock or futures contract is entered when using a limit order, this can be easily rectified by the client before the transaction occurs. The dramas arise when large 'at market' orders are placed and the trade transacts immediately in the market. In this case it is important to contact your broker promptly so attempts can be made to cancel the trade. Brokers can request a trade cancellation from the broker on the other side of the trade. Neither broker is under any obligation to do this.

> The trade can be cancelled if the client/broker on the opposite side agrees. They are not obligated to do this. Exceptions to this can occur. If the trade is at a price which doesn't reflect the current price range and is considered by the exchange to be 'unfair', then the exchange has the power to cancel the trade. These are referred to as 'busted' trades. If there is a large quantity involved the exchange may halt trading while the trades are cancelled and the orders are sent back to the market.
>
> Smaller operator errors are usually much easier to deal with. A client may, for example, place an order to buy one live cattle contract instead of one feeder cattle contract. Once the mistake is realised, the trader can simply reverse the trade by selling out of the feeder cattle and buying the live cattle. This may result in a small loss to the client, but has not caused too much grief in the market. In the share market if the trader had bought, say, RIO shares instead of CBA shares, the broker could ask to have the trade reversed and the orders reinstated.

Common trading errors

Regardless of the market or instruments being traded, many of the typical errors seen by brokers are the same. Interestingly enough, many of these errors are also the same as the mistakes discussed throughout this book. With education, attention to detail and awareness they can be avoided. Avoiding them will save you money and contribute to the successful operation of a profitable trading business. John Robertson reflects on the most common errors he has witnessed during his career as a 'local' on the floor of the Sydney Futures Exchange, a broker for a large brokerage firm, and now as director of his own brokerage business.

> Online platforms have enabled the investor to be part of the trading process. This attaches a personal and financial interest

to the placing and working of the trade which can interfere with what the actual trading plan is.

Human interference can create increasing problems. I worked the night desk in a big merchant bank in both Euro and USA shifts and if an error was made it was immediately handed over to another operator to exit. This removed the self-interest to the trade. Irrational thinking was removed.

Other important mistakes include the following.

ᗒ Having no money management (see chapter 8). This is by far the most commonly made mistake. Bad money management leads to overtrading (see chapter 18). *Traders need to count success in terms of a percentage return on their account, not the dollar value.*

ᗒ Averaging down (see chapter 15). This idea has killed more people's trading accounts than wars. If you buy a share at, say, $10, do not buy more at $8 when instead you probably should be getting stopped out of the trade.

ᗒ Traders not working stop losses or amending stop losses (see chapter 13). Don't be an ostrich and stick your head in the sand if a trade goes against you. When you place a trade work out where you will exit if it goes against you—and stick to it. Be disciplined.

ᗒ Trading thin markets can cause bad fills. Traders should always trade big markets with good trading volumes where it is easy to enter and unwind a position. The inherent risks of trading thin markets must be accepted before you place the trade.

ᗒ Not sticking to a trading plan (see chapter 3). Always know your rationale for a trade. Know your buy, stop-loss and profit target levels and stick to them. Writing these levels down for later reference is a good idea when getting started.

ᗒ Not knowing your market to the extent of not even knowing the correct market lingo. Global online platforms have increased traders' ability to access different markets. Each market has its own idiosyncrasies; learn them before you enter the market.

Specific examples of mistakes include:

▷ spread traders getting the legs around the wrong way; for example, 'buy soybeans/sell wheat' instead of 'buy wheat/sell soybeans'

▷ traders with small accounts trying to trade the big S&P500 contract when they should be trading the e-mini S&P.

Markets that don't trade 24 hours per day, six days per week make market on close (MOC) orders critical to get correct. Carrying a DAX position until next open can ruin your day if the market suddenly reverses or moves against you.

Avoid the grief

Many of these operational errors can be avoided through using common sense. Fully understand the markets you are trading and the platform you are using before diving in feet first. Below are some key actions that will help avoid many of these typical operator errors:

▷ Have a professional approach to your trading and the use of your online platform.

▷ Use the available demos and market simulators to test the platform and your trading system before using real money in the market.

▷ Become familiar with the use of the online platform so you can use it with confidence in the heat of the moment and during periods of intense activity.

▷ Know and understand the markets you are trading.

▷ Trade liquid markets.

➲ Start trading slowly and with small lot sizes until you build your confidence and execution skills.

➲ Have checks and balances in place; write down the trades and check them off as you execute.

➲ Stick to your trading plan.

➲ Respect the market.

➲ Use an online platform that validates your holdings and checks available funds before sending your instructions into the market.

➲ Use a platform that asks you to confirm the order before placing it into the market.

➲ Take your time. Mistakes are generally made when people rush. An extra few seconds to review the trade is hardly likely to ruin the trade, but a big mistake can.

John Robertson, founder of broking firm I-deal Financial Group Pty Ltd, began his trading career on the floor of the Sydney Futures Exchange way back when it was still an open outcry trading 'pit'. When the floor closed he made the transition to screen trader and then broker for Australia's largest futures brokers. In this chapter, John explained the pitfalls of operational errors and ways you can avoid them when trading.

John started I-deal Financial Group (<www.i-deal.com.au>) in 2006. The firm specialises in servicing clients using electronic trading platforms and auto-execution trading systems. He has extensive knowledge of the markets and trading in general, having experienced it all from both sides of the fence. His motto is: 'more markets, more opportunities'.

I'm sure I filed that somewhere ...

Mistake 20: avoiding the paperwork

Nothing is particularly hard if you divide it into small jobs.

Henry Ford

In addition to the daily activities associated with trading—scanning and analysing the market, entering and exiting trades, monitoring open positions, researching new ideas and systems—comes all the associated paperwork and record keeping. In many ways, this is the boring stuff. It is easy to delay it, avoid it, do other jobs and run away from it using any excuse you can find. However, it is an essential component of any trading business and one that must be completed on a regular basis. The more active your trading activities, the more work will be required to record results. Active short-term traders will obviously generate more paperwork, and have much more information to record and monitor than longer term traders.

Trader or investor

While tax laws will vary from country to country, most apply different tax treatment and legislation to traders than to investors. Tax laws and their interpretation can be complex. The ideas and concepts covered here are general in nature and should not be taken as specific advice. Individual traders and investors must seek out their own advice and opinion from tax professionals.

Don't be an ostrich

Having quantified that you are a trader, the importance of keeping adequate records of your trading activities then becomes a very important aspect of your daily, monthly, quarterly and yearly responsibilities. As well as for taxation purposes, the keeping of accurate records allows you to closely monitor the performance of your trading. It will enable you to calculate the important numbers discussed throughout this book. This allows you to determine the probabilities of your chosen trading system or strategy, and hence your 'edge' in the markets. Without understanding these numbers you will have no idea as to how you (or your system) are performing. You will also have no basis for comparison. If crunching these numbers is left too long or not done on a regular basis, then your trading business is either nothing more than a hobby or doomed to failure.

Sticking your head in the sand and avoiding the paperwork and record keeping associated with trading is not an option. You can only avoid doing it for so long until your broker lets you know you have depleted your trading capital to such an extent that you can no longer trade, your accountant starts screaming at you for paperwork to enable preparation of your tax return, or the relevant tax authorities come knocking on your door.

Jason Cunningham, a Certified Practicing Accountant (CPA) and founding member of Australian-based accountancy business, The Practice, offers some advice on the importance of keeping accurate records of all your trading activities.

> **The importance of good record keeping cannot be emphasised strongly enough. The right system of record keeping will aid in controlling trading finances. Without it, traders will not know**

how well or how poorly their business is performing. These records will provide important information on trading activities and assist with the preparation of income tax returns, business activity statements (BAS) and financial statements. From my experience, the five most common reasons traders avoid the paperwork are:

1. *It's boring and monotonous; there is nothing exciting about it.* It's easy to put it off for another day, and find other jobs to do rather than fill in another spreadsheet or form.

2. *Some people think it's not relevant*—trading is what they do so they don't want to spend time doing the menial tasks.

3. *It may uncover the 'hidden truth'*—that their trading is not profitable. So they avoid the paperwork to avoid the facts.

4. *Some people don't know how or where to start*—they are daunted by the scale of what they need to do, particularly if they have put it off for some time.

5. *One might have to pay tax if a profit has been made, so it's avoided it in an attempt to delay the inevitable.*

I've seen a situation where a client had a GST audit undertaken by the tax office on a BAS statement they had prepared where they expected to receive a GST refund. Because the client was unable to produce the appropriate paperwork (tax invoices) to substantiate their claim, the refund was knocked back and they were hit with a 25 per cent penalty.

Another guy got made redundant, rolled his super into a self managed superannuation fund (SMSF) and lost $200 000 in one year 'trading'. Perhaps if he had been more diligent with his paperwork he would have been more aware or accountable for the trading losses while they were still small and he may not have lost so much money.

Spreadsheets and computer programs

There are really no excuses for poor or inadequate record keeping. The ease with which information can be recorded in a spreadsheet (using software programs such as Microsoft Excel) makes it possible for anyone to be able to efficiently record all their trade results. There are also a number of purpose-built software programs available. All of these will allow you to record all aspects of all of your trades, including entry date and price, exit date and price, number of shares or contracts bought and sold, brokerage charges and profit or loss ensuing from the trade. More complex calculations to calculate win-to-loss ratios, average win versus average loss, and profit and payout ratios can also be undertaken. In short, every aspect of your trading business can be easily documented and recorded. These figures will provide you with all the information you need to determine the success or otherwise of your trading business. For share traders and investors, dividends received, share splits and mergers, and rights and bonus issues can also be recorded. In addition to the benefits of recording all this information for yourself it makes your accountant or tax agent's job in preparing your quarterly and annual tax returns much easier, and hence much more cost-efficient for you.

Making the recording of your transactions a daily activity is a great habit to get into. It is much easier to do it every day than to leave it to build up over a week or a month (or even longer). This is particularly important for more active traders who may have several trades to enter each day. Left to build up over a week, the task becomes daunting and keeps getting put into the too-hard basket, until it becomes an almost unmanageable job. It is a bit like the old 'a stitch in time saves nine' mantra that your grandma chanted all those years ago!

Online record keeping

For those using an online trading platform or a reputable vendor-supplied trading program, the job of recording all your trades and related information is made even easier. The majority will have an in-built function for recording all trades. Some of these online systems may be fully automated to the extent that the information is recorded automatically into this portfolio manager as trades are executed. Information on the overall performance of the system is continually calculated and available at the click of a mouse.

Backing up

The ever-present threat of computer malfunctions and 'bugs' makes it essential to back up all your information on a regular basis. As good as your spreadsheets and portfolio management software may be, it will all be of little use if your computer crashes and the information is lost. It is another good habit to ensure that you back up this information on a regular basis to an external source. This may be an external hard drive, memory stick, or CD ROM. It may also be an idea to send the information to your accountant or tax agent on a regular basis, as another way to ensure these records are kept offsite.

Pay a bookkeeper

If your trading system is short term, highly interactive and mentally demanding, then perhaps the last thing you want to consider at the end of the trading day is recording all the information from your day's trading activities. For those trading automated systems, this may not be an issue as you will have the time available to do it. If not, then a viable option may be to employ the services of a bookkeeper or data-entry person who can undertake this task for you. This is a relatively inexpensive option that will also ensure that the paperwork is done on a regular basis and in a timely manner. It may also act as another checking mechanism, as the bookkeeper will no doubt have questions and be checking all the relevant details. This will help ensure that any errors or discrepancies can be queried and sorted out early, rather than leaving them until it is too late or they have been forgotten about. Most brokers require you to check your trading statements within 24 hours to alert them to any discrepancies, incorrect fills or trades, or mistakes. Having an external third-party check through your trading records on a daily basis may well assist you in ensuring that these errors are identified and corrected early, before they become a larger problem.

Defining your activities — an Australian perspective

The following information provided by Jason is specific to the Australian regulatory environment. The definitions and rules will be different depending on your country or tax jurisdiction. Please take the time to thoroughly research and understand the tax implications for your trading or investing activities for the country in which you reside or trade. They will vary.

> Share traders are subject to income tax legislation. Investors' activities are governed by the capital gains tax (CGT) provisions of the *Income Tax Assessment Act 1997*.
>
> The main issue here is to determine whether your share trading activity can entitle you to be classified, according to the Australian Tax Office (ATO), as 'being in business' and therefore seen as deriving assessable income as opposed to generating 'capital gains'.
>
> If you are eligible to be classified as a business, you will be entitled to reduce your income tax commitments in three ways:
>
> ▷ Increase your entitlement to claim tax deductions.
>
> ▷ Treat shares as 'trading stock'. This allows you to value each share at the lower of cost or net realisable value, thus entitling you to account for any unrealised losses on shares without having to sell the stock, or close the position at the end of the financial year.
>
> ▷ If you've made a loss from trading throughout the year, you can offset that loss against other income—such as PAYG income from your employer if you were trading in your own name—which could lead to tax refunds.
>
> The situation differs if you were treated as deriving capital gains because:

▷ you can only offset capital losses against capital gains. If you've made losses throughout the year, you can carry them forward into future periods, but they can only be offset against capital gains not ordinary income.

▷ you are not entitled to account for unrealised losses. You can only recognise a loss once you have closed a position. This means that you may earn big profits in one year and a big loss in the next but still have to pay tax on profits earned in the profitable year.

To prove that you are in the business of trading you can either ensure you follow the ATO's guidelines and you self-assess, or you apply for a private binding ruling.

When self-assessing, the question of whether a person is a share trader or a share investor is determined on a case-by-case basis. The ATO will consider the following factors that have been used in various court cases:

▷ nature of the activities, particularly whether they have a purpose of profit making

▷ repetition and regularity of the activities

▷ the keeping of books and records and the use of a system, showing organisation in a businesslike manner

▷ volume of the operations

▷ amount of capital employed.

Note that the ATO has issued a fact sheet called 'Carrying on a business of share trading', which provides further explanation.

As the impact of this can be detrimental to your overall tax position, it is strongly recommended you seek the assistance of experienced professionals to assist you in determining whether you are a trader or an investor. Do not take a flippant approach.

If your situation is a bit doubtful, you have the option of applying for a private binding ruling. This process involves:

▷ completing the ATO-approved form

> ➽ attaching the appropriate commentary to substantiate your claim that you are 'carrying on a enterprise'

> ➽ linking your argument to the relevant public ruling, case law, tax determination and statute law.

Part of proving that you are in business is to register as a business. This is done by applying to the ATO for an Australian business number (ABN). An ABN is an 11-digit number that identifies you to the ATO and makes it simpler when dealing with most government bodies. It is at the discretion of the business owner as to whether they register for GST.

It is our experience that when trading, you are in business, and you should treat it like a business. The tax office rightly stipulates the guidelines for trading in a businesslike manner with a view to earning a profit.

Under the CGT regime, expenses cannot be deducted against capital gains. You can only offset capital losses against capital gains. However, this varies if you hold shares to derive dividend income, in which case certain expenses may be deducted against the dividends paid by those shares (for example, interest on a margin loan).

On the other hand, if you are classified as a share trader (or business), then basically all expenses incurred in deriving that income are deductible. The ATO's requirement is there must be a direct nexus or connection between the expense and the income. Therefore, deductible expenses can include the following.

> ➽ bank fees

> ➽ accounting fees

> ➽ interest on loans

> ➽ trading and investment courses

> ➽ books/literature/CDs

> ➽ internet expenses

> ➽ mobile phone and pager expenses

> ➽ data downloads

- ➤ cost of software

- ➤ laptop/PC

- ➤ car expenses (where applicable).

Essentially, these are the traditional expenses available to someone running a typical business.

To reiterate, due to the complexity of the taxation issues surrounding traders and investors, it is strongly recommended that you seek the assistance of an experienced professional to guide you through the myriad issues.

Shoes in a shoebox, records on a spreadsheet

With the technology and range of options available for record keeping, it is no longer acceptable or realistic to rock up to your accountant or tax agent at the end of the financial year with a box full of papers and expect them to miraculously produce a meaningful tax return for you. It is not even in your best interests. By constantly recording all your trading information and data on a regular basis you can constantly monitor your trading performance and have a firsthand knowledge of your performance. It also saves a significant amount on the cost of preparing tax returns and financial statements.

If you just turn up to your accountant with records in a shoebox, not only will you be charged an arm and a leg for the work, but chances are it won't be accurate. Plus, if you've registered for GST, you have to lodge a quarterly business activity statement (BAS), so it makes sense to prepare your records quarterly.

The other thing I'd like to stress is the importance of seeing an accountant to not only assist with your compliance obligations (such as tax return preparation), but to also get some proactive advice (such as tax planning and structure advice). It's also important to discuss these issues with accountants who understand trading and investing.

Jason Cunningham is a qualified CPA and financial planner with his own financial planning licence. In 1997, Jason co-founded an accounting firm called The Practice (<www.thepractice.com.au>), which provides accounting, taxation, business consulting, financial planning and finance solutions to a wide range of clients. In this chapter, Jason gave his valuable tips on how to stay organised—and profitable—when it comes to keeping records on your trading activities.

Jason has extensive experience in helping a wide range of clients grow and manage their financial affairs. A crucial part of his role—and the area he is most passionate about—is to help his clients identify and understand their needs and objectives, and give them the tools to reach their goals. Jason's specialty is the complex world of trading and tax. He has run numerous workshops and seminars for various share and option trading groups. Jason has a weekly radio gig tackling financial matters for callers. He is the author of *Where's My Money?*, a book packed with practical tools and real-life examples to help you take charge of your financial future and make your dreams a reality. This 10-step, plain-English guide has something for everyone—whether you earn $35k or $350k.

Glossary

anti-martingale system	a position sizing strategy that involves increasing position sizes as profits are made. *See also* martingale system
average true range (ATR)	the average of the 'true range' of price over a given period. The given period can be varied. *See also* true range
bad fill	occurs when a trade is entered or exited at a price different from that specified as a result of slippage
bear/bearish	a trader or investor who believes asset prices will continue to fall
bear market	a market with declining prices
black box system	a method of trading whereby the actual reasons for the trades are never known by the purchaser of the system
broker	a company or individual who executes buy and sell orders on behalf of clients

bull/bullish	a trader or investor who believes asset prices will continue to rise
bull market	a market with rising prices
busted trade	trades cancelled by an exchange if they are considered 'unfair' or not a true reflection of the prevailing market price
capital gains tax (CGT)	a tax due on profits realised on the sale of a capital asset, such as shares, bonds or real estate. Long-term gains on assets you own for longer than a year are taxed at a lower rate than ordinary income, while short-term gains are taxed at your regular rate. Assets held for over five years may be taxed at an even lower capital gains rate
commodities	physical products that are traded at a futures exchange such as grains, metals and meats
conditional orders	a buy or sell order that requires a specific set of conditions to occur before it becomes active in the market. These conditions may be price, time and volume related
contracts for difference (CFDs)	a share derivative allowing shares to be traded on margin
curve fitting	adapting a trading strategy to 'best fit' the historical data. This often produces performance results that are not able to be replicated into the future using actual prices and market conditions
day trader	any trader who consistently opens and closes positions on the same day
dividend yield	the theoretical return on an investment. It is calculated by dividing the dividend per share by the current share price, expressed as a percentage

dollar cost averaging	the practice of investing a fixed dollar amount at regular intervals (such as monthly) in a particular investment or portfolio, regardless of its price
drawdown	the amount of money lost on a losing trade, expressed as a percentage of your total trading equity
e-mini futures contracts	an electronically traded futures contract on the Chicago Mercantile Exchange that represents a portion of the normal futures contract. For example, the e-mini S&P500 futures contract is one-fifth the size of the standard S&P500 futures contract
exchange traded fund (ETF)	an investment vehicle traded on stock exchanges, much like stocks. An ETF holds assets such as stocks or bonds and trades at approximately the same price as the net asset value of its underlying assets. Most ETFs track an index
exit point	a predefined point at which a trade will be exited
fat fingers	a colloquial expression used to describe the incorrect entry of quantity or price when placing a buy or sell order
foreign exchange market (Forex)	the simultaneous purchase or sale of one currency against the purchase or sale of another
futures contract	an agreement to buy or sell a commodity or financial instrument at a specific price on or before a future date. These contracts are standardised according to the quality, quantity, delivery time and location; the only variable is price. Futures contracts are traded on various futures exchanges around the world

gearing	borrowing money to supplement existing funds in such a way that the potential positive or negative outcome is magnified and/or enhanced. It generally relates to using borrowed funds, or debt, to attempt to increase returns
indicators	mathematical combinations of price, volume and time parameters to aid in the technical analysis of financial instruments. Examples include moving averages, stochastic, relative strength and many others
intermarket spread	the simultaneous sale or purchase of a given delivery month of a futures contract on one exchange, and the simultaneous sale or purchase of the same delivery month of a futures contract on another exchange. For example, buying Chicago Board of Trade wheat, and selling Kansas Board of Trade wheat
intraday price swing	price movements within each trading day
investor	one who purchases an asset in the expectation of making a financial gain over the longer term
leverage	using small amounts of capital to control larger amounts of an asset. Using derivatives provides leverage
loan-to-value ratio (LVR)	The ratio of the loan amount for an asset to the market value expressed as a percentage
long/going long	buying shares or other assets in anticipation of a further increase in price. The assets can then be sold for a profit
margin	the amount of capital required to implement a trade in a derivative product

market if touched   an order to purchase or sell a security at the next available price as soon as a specific price is reached

martingale system   a position sizing strategy that involves increasing position sizes as losses are made. The classic model involves doubling the position size each time a losing event occurs. Normally used by gamblers. *See also* anti-martingale system

mechanical trading system   a specific set of rules that determine buy and sell decisions with the intention of removing emotion from both the decision-making and order execution process

moving average   a simple, or arithmetic, moving average is calculated by adding the closing price of the security for a number of time periods and then dividing this total by the number of time periods

moving average convergence divergence (MACD)   a trend-following momentum indicator that shows the relationship between two moving averages of prices

overtrading   excessive trading activity

position sizing   the number of shares, contracts or other instruments you will buy or sell. It is a function of risk profile, available capital and volatility

price-to-earnings ratio   calculated by dividing the share price by earnings per share. Used in fundamental analysis

profit target   a predefined exit target at which profits will be taken on a trade

R-multiple   profits expressed as a multiple of the initial risk. A 10-R multiple (sometimes referred to as a 10-bagger) is a profit that is 10 times the initial risk

R-value	the initial risk taken on any trade defined by the stop-loss
relative strength indicator (RSI)	an indicator based on the close-to-close price range that can be used to determine overbought and oversold conditions
short/selling short	selling shares or other assets you don't own in anticipation of a further fall in price. The assets can then be bought back again to cover the short position and a profit made
slippage	the difference between the price at which you expect to enter or exit the market and your actual fill price. For example, you may attempt to buy at $20 and be filled at $21—this is a $1 slippage
spread order/ spread trade	simultaneously buying one asset or trading instrument and selling another
stochastic oscillator	a technical indicator which compares the closing price to its price range over a given period of time. The belief is that in a rising market, prices will close near their highs, while in a falling market they will close near their lows
stock market index	a method of measuring a section of the stock market
stop and reverse	a trading method whereby trades are reversed when the initial trade is stopped out. For example, a trader who is long and gets stopped out immediately reverses the trade, and is now short
stop-loss	the price at which a trade will be exited if it fails to work out as anticipated. It is a risk management tool used to stop the losses from an open trade
system expectancy	how much you expect to make on average over many trades

target shooter concept	a method used by Larry Williams to calculate exits points for profitable trades. It is a feature of Trade Navigator software
thin market	a market with a low number of buyers and sellers. Prices are often more volatile and assets are less liquid. There is a larger spread between the bid and the offer price
tick chart	displays the minimum price moves (ticks) of a share or futures contract. Used by intraday traders
trader	someone who buys and sells financial instruments such as stocks, bonds and derivatives. Traders usually aim to catch shorter term price movements than an investor
trading system	a set of rules, including entry and exit points, money management and risk management rules for engaging the markets
trailing stop	the price at which you will exit a profitable trade that eventually reverses. The trailing stop price moves in line with the prevailing price trend
true range	developed by Welles Wilder, this indicator is a great tool for measuring volatility over a set period of time. It is defined as the best indicator of the distance from:

➣ today's high to today's low

➣ yesterday's close to today's high

➣ yesterday's close to today's low

volatility	a measure of the magnitude or speed of a price move over a given period of time. A market with high volatility will have large daily price ranges, while a market with low volatility will have small ranges of daily price

Index

FREE 30-DAY
TRADE NAVIGATOR
TRIAL

Let Trade Navigator give you the trading edge!

Simply type the following address into your browser and follow the instructions for your free 30-day trial of Trade Navigator software:

http://www.genesisft.com/trial/index.php?V=webwisdom

Your trial period gives you access to Trade Navigator software and all the market data you require to trial the program for 30 days.

Trade Navigator's training department provides you with one-on-one training and technical advice to help you get the most out of this gift—at no cost to you. Genesisft.com also has a large collection of online training videos and webinars for you to use at your leisure.

If you found this book useful...

...then you might like to know about other similar books published by John Wiley & Sons. For more information visit our website <www.wiley.com>, or if you would like to be sent more details about other books in related areas please photocopy and return the completed coupon below to:

P/T info
John Wiley & Sons Australia, Ltd
155 Cremorne Street
Richmond Vic 3121

If you prefer you can reply via email to:
<aus_pt_info@johnwiley.com.au>.

Please send me information about books on the following areas of interest:

- ☐ sharemarket (Australian)
- ☐ sharemarket (global)
- ☐ property/real estate
- ☐ taxation and superannuation
- ☐ general business.

Name:

Address:

Email:

Please note that your details will not be added to any mailing list without your consent.